I Like to Play

Carousel Readers

Adria F. Klein

Illustrated by Pam Posey

DOMINIE PRESS

Pearson Learning Group

I like to play with my dolls.

I like to play with my games.

I like to play with my dog.

I like to play with my cat.

I like to play with my brother.

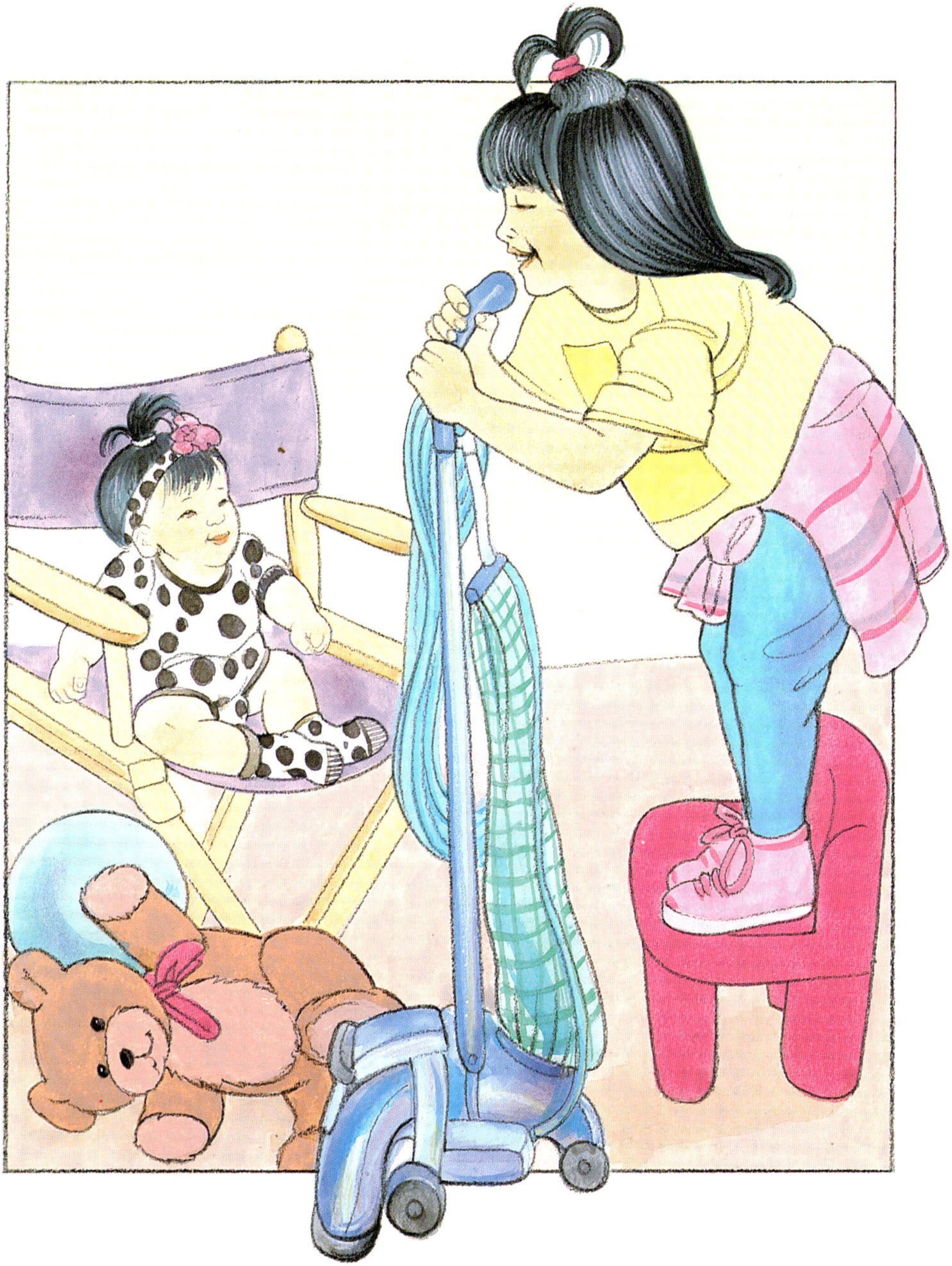

I like to play with my sister.

And I like to play with my friends.

Uncle

This is book one of a larger endeavor, Book of Saints

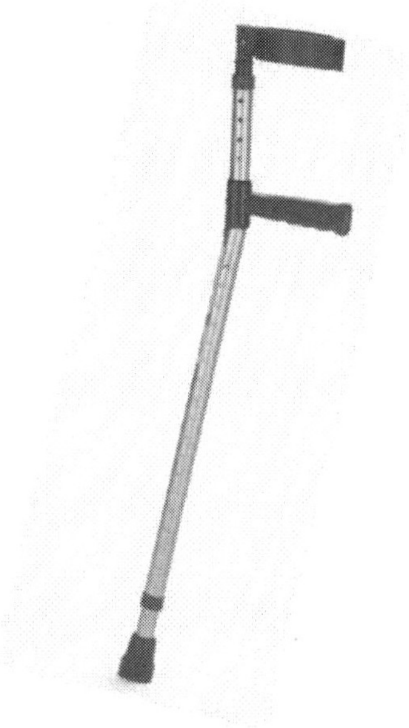

By: Dr. Vahid Hojreh

Edited by: Sam L Moya,

Jay Morganstern,

& Daniel Charles Wright

2 Dedications

I dedicate this work to my wife and family.

Thank you for supporting me in the beginning when I didn't show much hope.

Thank you for supporting me and being my rock.

To Ray's memory and friendship.

Cover art by: Cyrus Hojreh

ISBN: 979-8-234-06670-1

3 **Preface,** *The beginning*

To protect everyone involved, especially myself, this work is based on a true saint, but all characters are fictional. What follows is my version of the truth — a perspective that may not encompass the whole truth but reflects how I experienced it.

I heard about Ray's death from his son, Pa-yam. He called me on Thursday night. He said his father had been in too much pain for a long while. Then the phone crackled. Bad reception. My house had dead spots. I stepped outside by the garage door, but all I got was static. For ten seconds, nothing but broken words. I missed the moment he told me, but the truth of it was plain enough in the tone of his voice; Ray was gone.

I could have asked him to say it again, but I didn't. I couldn't. He had already said it once. That was enough.

Ray was dead!

Pa-yam gave me the time and place of the funeral. I didn't hear much of it. My mind was somewhere else. Ray and I sometimes had periods where we didn't speak. This was one of them. It had been over six months since I last talked to him. *Now I would never speak with him again, even though his voice has been with me consistently since his passing.*

I didn't go to the funeral. There were reasons, but none that matter now. I should have been there. But I wasn't.

That's partly why I'm writing this. Maybe to apologize. Maybe to make sense of it. Maybe just to put Ray's name down in ink, so he's still here, in some way.

Ray was a good man. Better than most. He saw the world in a way others didn't. I never got tired of hearing his perspective. I was never bored in his company. I will miss his bright outlook each and every day. 'Another day in heaven' was his greeting both when he answered the phone or if he saw you on the street.

In telling these stories, I hope something of Ray's soul and his quiet humanity comes through. If I speak of myself in this piece, it's only so you can know him better. I had to include my life to show you his.

The Following note is to Joy, Ray's wife and the boys:

Dear Amu Joon and Joy,

I am very sorry about your dad's passing, and I am truly sorry I was not there to mourn his passing in a traditional way with you. I can see why you might think it was not proper, and I understand that. I hope by writing this, I am honoring your dad's memory and paying homage to his beautiful soul and his love of life.

To Joy, I choose this name for you because you were the "joy" of Ray's life. We talked about everything in our lives; we were open to all kinds of topics between us. Many times, in private, he would acknowledge that you were his "angel", and he was more than blessed to have you as his wife and companion. He appreciated your undivided love and your unwavering support. You were always on his side and that gave him so much joy and reassurance.

I am also requesting your forgiveness—and your boys' forgiveness—for not being there during his burial and his sendoff. I just could not bear to be in a same room with some of his family members. I am deeply sorry for my absence, and I hope this letter can convey the respect and love I have for Ray and for all of you. With love, honor and regret.

Humbly yours,

Vahid

****

I have curated a collection of moments, stories, and memories of good and bad times—woven together like a collage of Ray, as seen through my lenses. Through these glimpses, I hope you, the reader, can experience what his nieces, nephews, and good friends saw in him. To us, he was more than just Ray; we affectionately called him Uncle Ray Ray. He was truly a "ray" of sunshine in our lives. I hope you enjoy.

6

First, *First impression*

I met Ray in my second year of college. I had tried to stay away from Iranians in general. Once, in high school, I had a bad experience. A boy who spoke my language but was not my friend ganged up against me so he wouldn't be the butt of the joke. I understood that he was making fun of me so he wouldn't be the target. Still the same, I tried not to associate with that type again. But Eraj was different. I met him at a Persian concert. He knew my cousin, so I trusted him.

He introduced me to another Iranian. Mohamad, though they called him Moe. He was short and stocky. Ray was his uncle, though they were only two years apart. That age gap was common in old Iranian families. My father has a nephew the same age as him. These things happened. We don't see families like that as strange.

Iranian names were made different now here in United States. During or soon after the hostage crisis, Iranians took American names. It was easier. It was

safer. I became Vinnie from Vahid. Mohamad became Moe. Reza became Ray. Some names were too common, like Ali or Mohamad, then an adjective or a noun was added to the name, sometimes a job or a description. Moe worked in a pizzeria. So, he became Pizza Moe, it was better than "Shorty Moe." Interestingly, later on, he opened a pizzeria called *Moe's Pizza*.

I had met Eraj a handful of times–few more times than Pizza Moe—when Moe asked me to play poker at his uncle's place.

I liked poker. I liked the game. I remembered my father and my uncles, sitting on the floor of our family room, laughing, playing. There was not much money. Just the joy of the game. Comradery. I watched them. I had listened to their voices, the joking, the cursing, the teasing. I wanted that. I wanted my own version of it. So, I happily agreed.

I put on my new Army style hemp jacket, which made me feel safe and warm, and I went. It was a long drive on a cold, wet autumn Friday night. Forty minutes all the way to New Brunswick. We all lived in the vicinity

Fifth, *The Good times, Camping*

No story about Ray would be complete without mentioning his love for camping. The outdoors meant everything to him. More than a sanctuary. It was the place where he let go of his anger. Where he healed. He intended to visit all the National parks in North America. Yosemite and Zion were his favorites. He recalled every landmark, road and vista. He intensely talked about them. With passion, fervor and love. Like old flames. Ray called himself Camp-man. Sometimes Abbott. Always going somewhere with meaning. Connecting to nature was his nourishment. Or was it another distraction from his pain? Or a delay in facing his demons?

Meanwhile, it was his wife who made the fire and laid out the gear and set up the tents. Ray would choose the place and the time. His job was to drive. He always had a destination, a plan and a date in mind. Every long weekend was accounted for.

of New York City and went to school in Newark. Moe, my cousin, Eraj, and I.

Ray was finishing his degree at Rutgers, the main campus. He lived with his mother. He was the last child. Five older sisters. His father had died when he was very young. I thought of my own father, the youngest of eight. Families had a way of repeating. I learned all that through Moe on the way there.

“There it is, that’s his place,” Moe pointed to the tallest building in the area. It was round or oval. It looked fancy from the backseat. Once we got there, it was just OK. Rent control for the elderly. Ray’s mother qualified and Ray had been freeloading on the couch for years.

When we arrived, no one was there, but Moe had a key. We went inside. There was very little furniture. The smell of cooked cabbage from the hall carried in. There wasn’t a table big enough for us, so we set up shop on the floor. Just like my father and my uncles had. We shuffled cards.

Still no Ray.

9

We opened beers and started without him. I thought it was strange, playing cards in a man's house before he even arrived. But it was all right. His nephew was here. That was enough.

We played. Fifteen to twenty minutes passed. I was leaning on a throw pillow with my head lowered and studying the three-card flop, I had a good hand. Then something landed in the middle of the pot. A cane with a big gray rubber stopper. *A crutch. Big. Shiny aluminum kind. My eyes followed upward, to the cane's owner. That was when I saw Ray for the first time.*

While I was eyeing him out, he pivoted on a crutch. He turned then hopped, one leg then the crutch. All of that while holding an open beer in his left hand. The right hand clasped on to the crutch tightly. He landed so gracefully on the ground, it was like watching a feather fall to the earth. It felt staged, as a ballerina dancing the Nutcracker, practiced a million times.

'Hi,' he said pleasantly. 'I'm Reza. Welcome.'

I was eighteen, younger than all of the guys. I had lived a small life. A careful life. I had never known a man with a disability. I had seen them, sure. On the streets. On TV. But I had never played cards with one. Never laughed with one. Never met one who was just a man.

Reza sat with poise. He did not apologize. He did not need to. Reza from the upper body looked like a typical southern Iranian man, dark features with a full 'Tom Selleck' mustache. The patches of hair on my own face hadn't even met yet. He looked more mature than everyone there, even my cousin, who was Reza's age. Ray, a real man, defiantly laid claim to who had the most testosterone among us.

He had come from work. Security. He had on pressed jeans and a company shirt stating his name, "Ray," on the left breast. He had to go back in an hour or so to hand over the keys to the next security guy. But for now, he played. We talked. He asked our names and what we studied.

I asked about his legs. The brace and the crutch. He shrugged.

'Polio,' he professed. 'When I was a kid. Legs didn't grow right.' Pause. 'Ever since, I've needed braces and one of these,' waving the crutch.

The brace locked at the knee to keep the leg straight, I observed. They unlocked with a switch, so he could bend at the knee. He needed them unlocked to sit. He then locked them straight to walk. That was how he operated.

Ray claimed to be 5 feet 5 inches. (More like 5'4"!) He always said without the polio, he would've been 5'8"—his father's height. He claimed it simply, without bitterness. Just the truth.

He lived with his mother. He said he is studying

Environmental science or something and meteorology. I forgot his major right away. Back then, if you were not an engineer you were not in my universe. He worked security jobs, 'it was easy to study on the job,' he would claim. Just enough to get by. He seemed content.

Ray had a very strong upper body, like a bodybuilder. That was what I thought. That was my first impression. He did not make a thing of his disability.

He played his cards. He drank his beer. He was not different. Not really.

Later, he laughed. 'I should be at work,' he said smiling. He was still on the clock. But he was here, playing poker.

He lost that job. One night, a bulldozer was stolen from the lot. He worked in a lot of heavy earth movers and construction machines. They just drove the bulldozer out of the lot with no one watching. They fired him for it. He didn't seem to care. But that was much later.

For now, we play poker.

Later, we played Guts! We played Guts after all the poker games. We decided it was a good way to win your money back if you had lost!

Rayisms:

Ray lived part of his life in the southern region of Iran, Bandar Abas, where he related to the costumes most. The southern people are stereotyped (correctly) as fun, great dancers, and good with women. Ray checked all those boxes. In that culture, one's Ray Ban sunglasses are one's most prized possessions.

In all of my times with Ray, I seen him lose his keys many times and his wallet a few times but never ever his Ray-Bans.

14

Second, *Chance meeting/ Ray as a Dad*

My impression of Ray did not change much for about a decade after I met him: “Admirable with questionable scruples.”

Perfect, much like me, and yet total opposites.

We saw each other now and then. Poker nights. Parties. Ray was there when we celebrated my college graduation. It coincided with my letter of invitation to try out for the old MLS team called the NY Cosmos. I never went. I had injured my right knee’s ACL just before.

Our connection was nothing deep, nothing lasting. He was not my close friend. I did not even have his number. If I needed to reach Ray, I called Moe, his nephew. That was the way of things. We lost touch. Meanwhile, he left for Dallas, got married, went through a big surgery on his back and neck and had a son. I did not find this out until years later.

15

I was leaving New Jersey myself, one of the last from the original gang. Eraj had gone to California years ago. Then, Ray went to Texas. Then Moe. Now me heading west to Arizona.

I drove to Phoenix in December 1994, in my car full of everything I owned. I stopped in Dallas on the way for two nights. Moe was there. I stayed with him and his wife, whom I had never met. She was nice I remember.

We went to a Persian restaurant the next day, in the afternoon. I slept in late. Ray was there. He asked me a thousand questions about my move to Phoenix. He wanted to know what it was like. I found it a bit strange at the time. He invited me to his home to meet his family later that night. Meanwhile, the restaurant's food was just ok. I'd had better. It made me gassy.

I went. The house was warm and something smelled yummy even though I was full. The Christmas decorations were up. Neither Ray nor his wife were Christian, just like many Iranians, they celebrated Christmas for the kids. His boy was small, maybe

three or four years old. Pa-yam ran through the house with a screwdriver. A Phillips head. He held it tight. I watched him, ready to grab it out of his hands. Ray raised his hand to stop me, then reaffirmed that it was fine. The boy unscrewed appliances and broke them sometimes. Ray claimed that it would teach him not to fear machines. His son would learn to solve problems, to build, to fix. It was strange, but it made sense at the time. I had never heard of such a thing, and I never forgot it. I inquisitively questioned, "you worried about him getting electrocuted?" while his son was unscrewing an electrical outlet. Ray shrugged it off "he'll learn."

Ray was a different kind of father.

A month later, Ray was in Phoenix with his family for a visit. He shrugged when I asked why. Just a road trip, he claimed.

Less than two months after that, he moved 15 minutes from me. He liked the Phoenix area, he said. Later on he confessed that intra-family relations in Dallas was getting toxic for his wife and himself. That was when we started to become very close.

He had driven a thousand miles to see if Phoenix could be home. And now it was.

***Rayisums**: Ray had polio. His left leg was braced, cast in iron. His right leg could bend at the knee, but only if he unlocked it. Driving was his freedom. Ray could drive well—if he cared to focus. Most of the time he didn't. He liked his pipe too much. He smoked while driving. Packed it, lit it, and sometimes cleaned it, all while we were moving down the road. It made me nervous to sit next to him. But he liked the pipe. He insisted that it calmed him and helped him with the pains. His right leg with the locking mechanism, needed to be unlocked to break, every time. It was slow. Too slow, I would fear many times. But he made it work.*

Third, *Story of Ray's nature*

It was early March. The mornings were still cold, though the sun came up strong. I was working a half-day shift that Saturday downtown. Ray had moved into town. He called and offered, "Let's go for a drive. Let's explore".

Meandering became our signature pastime.

Ray liked to drive. He always had. That was his way of getting close to the world or to run away. I hadn't lived in Phoenix long. Maybe three months. I knew a few people, but not many. So when Ray called, I went. I always went. It was good to have a friend in the city.

During the years to come, we had been on a lot of drives. Some of them were long and hot and foolish. Once, he got us stuck in the sand out in the desert, in July, with a little car that had no business being there. That was a hard day.

But this day was different. He picked me up from work. There was someone sitting in the front

passenger seat. I got in the back without asking. That's how it was with Ray. Things didn't always come with explanations.

I said hello. Ray turned and finally announced, "This is Jim. Jim, meet Vinnie." More enthusiastically, he continued, "Jim here is a vet. He is down on his luck. We're taking him north, as far as we can, so he can catch a ride to Flagstaff."

So, we drove north, and I listened. I listened to Jim talk about his life and the things he had seen in the war, Vietnam, and after. And I thought about Ray. A man with a limp, always with a grin, not afraid of picking up someone off the side of the road. That struck me. That stayed with me.

It wasn't just Jim I was learning about. It was Ray, too. I had thought I knew him—from poker nights and short talks here and there—but I didn't. Not really. Not like this.

We stopped at a Waffle House off Route 17. The weather was changing. It was getting windy, with more clouds rolling in by the minute. Ray pulled into the lot. He parked and pulled some dollars from his

pocket. Then he looked back at me in the rear-view mirror, over his Ray-Bans and forcibly inquired, “You got anything you can spare?” I gave Jim a twenty. Ray smiled and continued, still looking over the shades. He did a little tilt of his head backward. “Hey, isn’t that your old jacket from College?” he paused, “The forecast for Flagstaff is snow for tonight”.

This may be a good place to share something I learned from him on that drive. Even though Ray worked for years for an Environmental company in Dallas, he got his degree in meteorology!

It was the same jacket. I am frugal that way. An old Army jacket I’d had for over fifteen years. I wasn’t going to need it much longer in Phoenix. Ray didn’t say it outright, but I knew what he meant. I only pause for a second. Then I reached into the pockets, it felt like it wasn’t mine anymore, took out what belonged to me, and handed my trusty cover over to his new owner, Jim. Silently saying goodbye to my beloved jacket, my shield.

That was Ray. He didn’t just give a man the shirt off his own back. He made you give yours, too. And

somehow, you didn't mind. Somehow, it felt right. That was Ray. This was not an unusual story for Ray, that was just the first time I saw it.

Rayisms: *Have you ever been in line behind a person that is having a personal conversation with the cashier, and you are tapping your foot, checking your watch, waiting? That was Ray talking away, he always wanted to 'spread the cosmic cheer' to everyone, he had a ready but sometimes not willing audience in servers and cashiers!*

Fourth, *A picture of Ray's character*

I was lonely in that town. It was the kind of loneliness that doesn't go away just because people are around, too. It was the kind that sets in your bones and stays quiet until late in the night. Then Ray moved in, and the feeling changed. We were everywhere together. We drove long stretches of road. We talked for hours. We created several code words between us two. We talked about things most people don't. Things that sit heavy inside your heart and are hard to say out loud. We talked about 'what ifs.' We talked about fear. Real fear. The kind that keeps most men awake. We planned a trip to the Grand Canyon whenever things got too much, and we needed to run away from it all. We mentioned it to each other to cope with stress and pain. We didn't always come to answers, but talking to each other helped.

Ray became a part of my life. And I learned his. He was the youngest of six. The six who lived. His father died when Ray was just a year old. His oldest sister

was trying to make it through nursing school. In the chaos of all that grief of losing her father, she missed something important. Ray never got his Polio vaccine. And the disease found him.

It hit the joints of his legs hard, mostly the left. After a few surgeries, he wore a full brace on the left leg a partial on the right and needed a crutch to walk. It never seemed to slow him down, but I could tell it hurt. He never liked to talk about the pain with others unless it was part of a story, and his stories were purposeful and timely. I tried to learn from his bravery. During that time, my neck and shoulder were causing me much pain and even kept me from sleeping, but I tried to keep it to myself.

By the time I met him, Ray had been through more surgeries than I could count. Operations on his back, his hips, even his neck. Over the years we lost touch. He moved to Dallas and had another major surgery. They placed a rod to keep his spinal cord from bending anymore. They used a lot of hardware. Ray had pain in his bones; they couldn't fix that. He admitted that the surgery was the hardest thing he had ever gone through. He maintained, "If I had to do

it again, I wouldn't. I'd just end it." And when he said it, he wasn't dramatic. He just confessed it like a man who knew the edge and had looked over it. He spent weeks in a rehab center after that. But he didn't complain. Just claimed, "It had to be done." He lived with pain most of the time. He didn't like the medicine the doctors gave him. Claimed it made his mind foggy. So, he turned to herbs and plants. Tea, and smoke. He insisted they helped, and I believed him. He managed the pain by layering various methods. Alcohol, smoke, and then pain meds.

Ray's upper body was impressive. Not just strong but shaped by effort. He kayaked in the ocean. He went white water rafting. He'd drive with his kayak strapped to the roof of his Subaru, always ready to find a new body of water. He liked movement. He liked nature. It silenced his inner demons. That was my theory.

Later, Ray designed and built his own hand-powered bike. By himself, he made a CAD model and engineered the whole thing. He worked with some welders to make it real. The bike was sharp. Even though it was made from mismatched parts all from

different manufactures pieced together. Much like Dr. Frankenstein, he pieced it together, and it worked. It worked smoothly and clean. He made his creation foldable of course, so he could fit it in the back of his Subaru Outback. He amazed me. Ray liked to bring harmony into the chaotic world, if he could somehow control it. Now he'd ride with his hand bike for miles. Alone. Just him and the road. He loved it. No longer looking hard for water, he could kayak in. Now all roads were his place of worship, his meditation.

I discovered early that Ray always offered to drive. He loved to drive. Every time he drove, and we found ourselves needing to park, he never parked in the handicapped spots. Even though he is clearly qualified.

I asked him <u>once</u> at the beginning, "Why don't you park there, Ray? You've got the tag," pointing to a handicap spot next to the entrance.

He looked at me. Quiet for a second.

Sounding disappointed, he reminded me, "There are people out there who need it more than I do."

That was how he lived. Not with big words, but with choices. Not with speeches, but with quiet dignity. He didn't ask for much. He didn't expect much. But he gave plenty. And if he had something to offer, he gave it without needing to be seen.

That's the kind of man Ray was. And I was lucky to have him as my best friend.

***Ray history**: Ray wore black jeans almost every day. Not one pair—several. All pressed sharp creases like blades. Shirts, too. Sometimes T-shirts, sometimes button-ups. But it was always the same style. I thought it was just a habit. Later, I learned he had several black jeans in the closet all pressed. His wife, Joy, pressed them and helped him get dressed each morning. His fingers didn't work. The hands looked strong, but the joints were stiff. No dexterity. He couldn't do buttons.*

I asked, "Why wear button-ups at all?"

He admitted, "Because I can take them off easier. And she helps me."

He declared it without an apology. She helped him with that. She helped him with it a lot. Every day. And he never spoke of her to me without professing that she was an angel. He was lucky, and he knew it.

When I got engaged, things moved fast. My fiancée came to live with me in July, and we needed to make it official, for the elders in the family. So, we got married at a mosque in Tempe. It wasn't a big wedding. It was a way to live together until we could have a full ceremony.

I gave everyone less than a week's notice. Still, my future father-in-law flew in from L.A. My uncle, who lived nearby (part-time), came to stand for my side. And of course, Ray.

Ray showed up in a full suit. It was August 3rd. Phoenix in August is often cruel—hot and humid. He had his shirt buttoned to the top and a tie that matched. He told me later it took him over forty minutes to dress. His wife helped him of course. He seemed uncomfortable and, as always, in pain. But he showed up, dressed sharp. And he was on time. Maybe for the first time. He did it for me: that was special.

All that and I hadn't even asked him to dress up.

My first time camping in Arizona was with Ray and his family. It was at Lake Mary's campsite, very large. Elevation 7,000 feet. Early in March. I didn't know what I was in for. I accepted their invitation, knowing that I had no camping gear. I'd left it all back East.

We were the only ones at the whole campsite! No one else in the state seemed that brave or foolish to be there at that time. It snowed that night, light dust but very cold and windy. I lay there in their tent, shivering, thinking I'd surely freeze. I heard things in the middle of the night, rustling. It wasn't the wind that made me concerned and alarmed. I counted the minutes before first light. At dawn I headed for the door with a zipper. That's when I saw the tracks. A lynx. Ray identified it later. It had come by in night. Walked to, and around our tent. Ray probably heard it too. He is a light sleeper. He probably heard it but didn't care. We camped many times after that. Too many to count. Always with his family, and then with mine. But never in the snow again.

Like the way he did most things, Ray always walked with purpose. He noticed many things. Walking with him, where he'd stop in his tracks and call you over,

was a common occurrence. *"Come here, look at this." A plant or a flower, even a rock. He loved nature.* Geology and Earth Sciences were his hobbies. Ray would notice treasures that most would walk by. He lived in the moment. The Now. Ray saw nature in a different way. He saw it as if it were speaking to him. And he listened. We would sit for hours on a rock at a vista, just listening to the wind.

We went to Zion, Arches and Bryce. Good trips. Great nights of laughter and stargazing. But Yosemite—that was his place. As previously mentioned, camping with Ray meant he wasn't about to help. Not with the tents or the fire. He would drive around and spot firewood, though. He would leave all other tasks to others, mostly his wife. But he was the best companion to sit with under the stars. He'd point at the stars and tell you something worth remembering. Always something worth remembering.

Every night before he went to his tent to sleep, he'd walk to the fire pit. And relieve himself in it. Ashes flying everywhere. The distinct sound of liquid drizzling on the hot coals! Then the smell, ugh! That was Ray too. Unapologetic.

Rayisim/ history*: Ray didn't speed nor tailgate. I give him that. He drove calmly, most of the time, in Arizona, when I drove with him. He was decent behind the wheel. But back in Jersey, it had been a different story. Too many violations. Too many points. They suspended his license. He ignored it. The Arizona DMV found out eventually. AZ Motor Vehicle Dept. sent him many letters. He ignored those too.*

******

Being Ray's friend meant being there. Anytime. Three a.m. Four. Five. He'd call. Sometimes it was his wife. "Is Ray with you?" she'd plead. I was his alibi. He used me, and I never minded. That's what best friends do.

******

One early morning, I got a call at 4 am—he was in jail. A traffic stop. They ran his license. It wasn't valid. They arrested him. I had to bail him out.

He was laughing when I picked him up. "That was something," he confessed smiling. "Interesting people in there. One guy was growing pot. Another was a gang member. I might write a book about it." He almost looked giddy. It seemed like he was sad to leave. He mentioned that night in jail as if it was just another adventure. The twelve hours he spent there were just another chapter for him. He later told me little pieces, character by character.

Ray never brought up the Grand Canyon that day. That surprised me. He usually did after a long, stressful episode. But not this time.

If you knew Ray, none of the driving stories would surprise you.

Sixth, *The tough times/ Big Surgery*

The big rod that they placed in Ray's back a decade ago, the one supporting his spinal cord from bending even more, had broken. It was also the anchor for his neck. That long metal rod held the rest—the bolts and the pins, all the way up to his spine. That rod had fractured. Now it needed to be replaced! Ray needed another posterior spine fusion. Ray was in for a lengthy recovery!

That was Ray's greatest fear. Not the pain. Not the danger. The recovery. The months of rehab. He had gone through too many surgeries. He didn't want to do it again. Would he be the same after it? He lost some of himself with every surgery. How much will remain after this one? As much as he tried to control life, life fought back.

But he had no choice. Ray needed to see his boys grow to become men. He wasn't giving up yet. I was good to commiserate with, since my shoulder and

neck's severe metallic-like pain had escalated. It was now affecting my work. I was also seeking surgical solutions.

Through his sister's connections and some doctor friends, they got him into a great hospital. In Los Angeles. One of the best. The surgery was long. Close to twenty hours. They removed the old hardware and put in a new rod. They worked hard. The doctors and nurses did their part.

Ray sent me his final X-ray. I wish I had kept it. Some with over two hundred screws and bolts. Rods and pins everywhere. It didn't seem real. But all that metal was inside him.

I visited him when I could. During work breaks, I went to California. I saw him in a hospital bed. I helped with his therapy a few times. We tossed a balloon. Caught it. Toss it back again. He had to teach the muscles how to work, from the beginning. Just to catch and throw. To relearn to walk and, most importantly, to drive again. The surgery would give him more time on the planet. For many more years, we all hoped.

Ray was never the same after that surgery. He never rode his kayak nor the hand-bike he built. After that surgery, he started using a wheelchair. Before that, you couldn't catch him dead in one, he despised them. But now he needed the wheelchair. He even started to park in the handicap spots. "I need the room to swing my door open and get my chair out," he professed, as if someone had inquired. But no one had. He needed a steering wheel spinner knob, installed in his car to make turns. But he could drive again. Ray would have died if he could not at least drive.

As Ray was close to the edge again we started talking about the Grand Canyon much more after that surgery. The scenario had changed a bit; now I had to help with his wheelchair, help him navigate the trails.

A few months after rehab, Ray did something I had never seen him do before. He had me and another friend act as his handlers to get better seats in a concert. We used the handicap section at a crowded Pink Floyd concert. A sold-out show.

A glimmer of fear was now showing through the first cracks of his stoic exoskeleton. To succumb and accept accommodation for a handicapped person was unlike him. He was losing control.

I see it clearly in hindsight now. After that surgery, he started to see himself as handicapped. Disabled. In need of help at times. That was the first for him.

Ray history: *I called Ray and his wife to stay abreast of his surgery, time and location. I soon went to visit. I talked to him before leaving and his only request was his pipe and some weed! I asked him how in hell are you going to use it in the hospital, if I bring it?*

He calmly answered, "Leave that to me, I know what I am doing!".

I did and he did! Ray never ceased to amaze me.

37

Seventh, *Breaks in the Line*

For over twenty years, Ray and I were friends. But there were a few estranged periods between us. Sometimes he'd get mad. He'd stop talking to me. Just like that. My wife would say, *'He's like your girlfriend. Full of drama.* And maybe she was right.

There is a mentality in Persian culture, that is: in the process of getting to know someone, you are allowed to create scenarios to test your subject. I had issues with most Iranians from the beginning due to this. It's something of a habit with most who spent their formative years in Iran.

Ray would often tell me that I failed him. He'd go silent for months. Six, seven, sometimes more. It was never clear why. Either what I did or failed to do, struck a nerve with him. He would stop calling me, and my calls would go straight to voicemail. Then something small would pass between us. An email. A birthday. A bit of news. The ice would crack, and we'd

be back. But the reason for the silence was always left behind, unsaid.

Ray was incommunicado during his wife's cancer treatment. He was a supportive husband. He stepped up and took care of the family during that time. He was upset with me and my wife's level of support for her.

After a while, I stopped trying to figure it out. I cherished the time I had with him. Most times I would think twice before telling him things that he may misinterpret. That was Ray, though on the outside but ultra-sensitive heart.

Ray's history: *At the beginning of our friendship, Ray stopped all communications and planned camping trips because I failed to rescue him 45 minutes away in North Phoenix. He had lost his keys. He called my house, but I had important dinner guests and wouldn't answer. He knew that too. He knew I had guests that I was trying to impress. I was preparing for that night for weeks. I think he was testing me. My wife thinks he got jealous of our guest. I ended up cutting*

the dinner short and drove up to rescue him and his family, but I did not find him. Who knows exactly what happened, but he did not speak with us for a good six months after that. I think he finally took a cab home. Years later I tried to bring it up and help heal our relationship, but he dismissed my reasoning.

Eighth, *Hunting Past/ Ispahan*

This and the next chapter were the hardest to write. First because it's a somber topic, and second, I must reveal so much of myself for this story to make sense to the reader. I am trying to stay in the shadows in Ray's chronicle and have him shine. But without revealing my history here I cannot achieve the overall goal.

My oldest son was about eight when I first started to fully remember what had happened to me when I was a young boy. I had the misfortune of being sexually abused by a family member. It was a major psychological wound. I was eight and a half. I had buried it in a corner, down deep. Shut it off. The mind has a dark place for that. You don't see it, but the poison works at you all the same. It was like a dream that repeats and torments you, though you don't remember it.

Then the memories all rushed back like a tsunami the day my wife let our son sleep over at his friend's

house without checking with me. She meant no harm. But I fought back. I yelled. I raged. I made a scene like a man protecting something—but I did not know what "IT" was I was protecting. It wasn't about the sleepover. It was something old and rotten. Something that had happened when I was about my son's age. Something I had never fully faced and processed.

It took time to remember the details. It took time to see it all. It took more time to label it. Years, maybe. But when I started to let go of the hurt, I knew it. I began to heal. Slowly. The way a man heals after a deep wound.

After a decade, I forgave. I stopped feeling the blame. I forgave my parents, myself, and others. That part was the hardest, but I did it. The shame had dissolved. The process of healing has been my greatest success in life. The pride that I still carry to this day, for overcoming that invasion, is by far my greatest accomplishment, even more than any monetary or academic achievements I have attained. It took many self-help books. It took a kind of labor no one sees. Looking back now, I know I should have

asked for help along the way. But the shame... Men often think they must do things alone. I thought that too.

I told Ray about it. Not at first. Not even years later. It was a few months before my shoulder replacement surgery. Ray was fresh out of his physical therapy. He was operating at seventy percent; he was mending. Stronger. He was driving again. He was living near San Diego now. Closer to his surgeons. I went to see him when I could.

In this particular meeting, we sat on the concrete bench on the edge of a cliff, overlooking the ocean, near Dana Point. The beach and the crowd were far below. Lila was Ray's new service dog there. Gentle and full of joy.
She was the first dog I ever loved.

Soon after, my wife and I would get one of our own. Ray taught me how to raise our dog. How to housetrain her. The way a friend would pass on what he knows. When he met my dog a year later, he was surprised by my dog's good behavior.

43

There on the concrete bench, we sat. We shared a pipe. The wind was controlling but gentle. The ocean looked ominously calm, yet powerful. The world looked very tranquil in that way it can be when two men have been reunited in their stories of pain. That day was early summer. A good day. The kind of day that makes you feel strong and brave. Maybe it was my upcoming shoulder surgery that made me so forthcoming. Maybe it was just the right time, or maybe I thought Ray was strong enough to hear my encounter with my past.

We sat there for a while, listening to the wind, watching it play with the leaves. There were never awkward silences between us. We had often spent hours, happily without words. The waves' rhythmic and consistent meeting of the rocks was calming and reaffirming. So, I started to tell him. After years of self-work and stacks of books read, I felt strong enough to just say it without getting emotional. I was proud of that. Just like ripping off a Band-Aid, I just said it. I told Ray the saga of being raped in my own closet when I was eight.

Ray was quiet for a long while. I was waiting for his response. I don't recall breathing for a long while. His pause was longer than it should've been. On the edge of my seat, pretending to be calm. He finally moved. He made a decision, it seemed. Slow and deliberate, he turned to look at me. It was tough moving his neck that way. He was still healing from the surgery. Finally, with half-raised eyebrows, his voice soft and kind. In a whisper, he pronounced, "Oh. You too!".

That was all. Just those words.

I had thought I would be the one to surprise him. To shake the air between us. I thought maybe he'd offer comfort. But instead, he dropped a bomb. It shocked me to the core.

I sat there stunned. Then the questions came in fury.

"What do you mean, *you too*?" "What happened to you?". "When?"

I didn't know too much about Ray's inner family dynamic. Only what he had offered to share. Only what a man lets his best friend know.

Ray had shared a story a while ago about him being sent away to Isfahan. A disabled ten-year-old was sent away to a boarding school, out of town.

Ray enlightened me about the circumstances which he lived with in that boarding school. He emphasized, "Think about it, me ten-eleven with a crutch in Isfahan, with minimum supervision!"

I thought about that. A ten-year-old boy. A boy with a limp. A kid who moved slowly and carefully. A young boy with a brace on one leg needed a cane to walk. He can't run away! Ray was sent to a place full of other maturing young men. Some of which are older and more sexually advanced. Wild boys with eyes sharp like knives and no one watching them.

It turned my stomach.

He vented, "My big sister sent me to that place and left me there for two years!"

Maybe he was sent away so the family feels less ashamed of their past oversight.

He did not divulge much more. He did not have to. I saw it. I almost felt and smelt it. Like a dark shadow behind a curtain that takes a form, it all came

together. I had been there. The same place Ray was talking about. His house of horrors. I shivered at the resurrecting memories.

Ray knew I was born in Isfahan. I knew he had gone to school there. Later, we discovered that we were both at the same compound. I think it was over a campfire when we discovered that.

His boarding school had closed and then became my temporary elementary school while my school was being rebuilt after a large storm damaged the old roof. I went to the new location in September. Ray had just left his school in May. The same complex that was now my new temporary school. I was nine. Ray must have been 11 when he left. I was there just a few months after Ray left. I remembered the place well.

Most large homes or structures in the desert—Isfahan is on the edge of a desert—were designed in a U-shape, facing north with a large courtyard. This was a way to stay cool without air-conditioning. In this school the courtyard was the size of three football fields with classrooms all around. A lot of the rooms were locked. We only used the most northern rooms. The classrooms were old. So much cricking, stale old

air hung in the rooms. There was a large empty field by the classrooms with a huge tree in the middle, that's where we mostly played. Then there was an acre or two densely packed, thin trees closer to the entrance of the school, very odd!

It was not like other schools. I couldn't put my finger on it then, but this new school seemed sinister, layered with hidden histories. There were many strange parts to school. There was a bathhouse! I saw it once. It was usually locked up. Let's not forget the small woodsy part in the middle of the property. One could find all kinds of reading materials loosely buried. Playboys and such. One kid found an old condom. We didn't know what it was. We were in Elementary school after all. But we knew it was dirty. The whole place felt eerie and dark. We didn't know that our new school used to be a boarding school for older boys.

Most of the old classrooms were locked. Some had double and triple bunk beds stacked against the walls. We used to sneak in through windows. Boys do that. We'd sneak in and explore the locked rooms. The sleeping quarters were still there. The memories of

that place were haunting and now vivid. I remember the air. It smelled old, dirty and moldy. Like rust and dust and sweat that never dry. There was darkness in those rooms. Something evil lingered. It was on the walls and furniture.

I remember standing in the middle of one of those rooms, gazing at one of those bunk beds, a chill went through me, back then, when I was 9. I felt a coldness that didn't come from drafts and leaky windows. It was the frigid hand of evil. I never went back to those rooms. Even as a boy, I knew not to.

Now, sitting beside Ray on that cliff above the ocean, with his dog at our feet, I saw it all again. That room. That bunk bed. Maybe it was Ray's!

I shivered once again!

Ray was being gang raped night after night. "They took turns till I started to bleed" Ray confessed whispering. He spent almost two years in that hell hole!

I was proud of myself for telling the story without breaking. I had gone over the words in my head a dozen times. More. I had smoothed it out. Made it

clean. Made it bearable. And I told it. But I wasn't ready for his story and his response. Not the way it came. Quite surprised and in shock. I started to tear up.

I hadn't planned on that. I was the one telling *my* story. I was the one with the weight to carry, the pain to speak. I had shaped it into a thing I could say aloud.

But his story cut through all that. His few words had magically changed the weather around us too. Clouds rolled in, it got overcast fast and the breeze had turned to a gust. The waves were now crashing the rocks to the rhythm of my pounding anger.

We both had been violated in the same year, same city, Isfahan. Ray in that school and I, in my closet. "How do you deal with the memory, the pain". I asked him, trying to make sense of it all?

Ray looked at me, side eyed, and suggested, "Dude. That was the past. Live in the now. Life is a blessing and so beautiful." He continued "Spread Cosmic cheer, many people need it." He declared as if he'd been absolved from all his sins, or had forgiven all of theirs. He meant it. Every word.

I was thinking then, how is it that my experience made me hard and resentful? It took a decade to repair the wounds, yet Ray's experiences made him a kinder and gentler man. It had left him loving people and life, spreading cosmic cheer wherever he went. How? How is that possible?

As if he had heard me ask, or by chance, while his soul visibly shimmering through the facade of his physical body, he answered:

"'...the wound is where the light comes in' Rumi".

Ray's influences: *One of my favorite activities with Ray was staying home, reading, and discussing Persian poetry. Since he was older and had more schooling in Iran he had a better command of the Persian language. Ray would read and help me with the meaning of tough, long words. He got me into Sohrab Sepehry and Rumi and helped me understand other famous Persian poets, Khayyam and Hafez.*

My three sons' middle names are Rumi, Sohrab, and Hafez.

Ninth, *Grand Canyon, a landscape to die for*

The last time Ray reestablished communications after another gap in our amaranthine friendship, I visited him in San Diego. It was a short visit. Strange, looking back on it now. It came not long after my shoulder surgery and rehab. My right shoulder was articulating bone on bone. It was the degenerative kind of rheumatoid arthritis. The whole articulating capsule was shot, which led my shoulder to dislocate often. My neck, too, was causing shooting pains. Work had worn me down. I was in pain most of the time. A long way from possibly playing pro-soccer.

I quit working. The pain in my neck began to normalize just a bit. But it was after the shoulder surgery that I began to improve. It took over a season to be operational. I was sleeping better, finally. I was lighter. Happier. Hopeful. I started to meditate regularly.

Ray and I used to talk about our pain. It was something we understood together. Something we

shared. I told him that I was doing much better. I thought he'd be happy. I thought it might give him hope. But he wasn't overjoyed. Not the least. But he acted as if he was, like a good friend.

Looking back, I think he felt left behind. Ray had lost a brother-in-arms. A partner in pain. Why wasn't I wise enough then? I was not spiritual enough to see his hurt. To feel his loneliness hiding behind the act. I wish I had seen it more clearly, then. Ray was chained to his pain and lost control.

We spoke many times after that. We said many things. But not once did he bring up 'Grand Canyon' to me again. Not after that conversation.

****

Before his second big surgery in LA, while his pain was getting worse, we commiserated about our aches often. During those times, there were only a few ways for Ray to feel better. The layering of drugs was his go-to path. Alcohol, weed, and a couple of Oxies to get through a day. I hate to admit it, but talking about our pain had added a new layer of bonding between

us. Not many people around us know the severity of our sufferings.

I know I was going through a fraction of what he was feeling. But still, at times, the pain was unbearable for me. I couldn't handle it, never mind Ray. When he and I both got too overwhelmed by our physical torments, we thought up ways of ending "It." It was a dark and ghoulish pastime.

We both had kids. We needed a good way to depart without harming their psyche much more. It would be best if we just passed naturally or accidentally. We thought about all the different types of exits. We discussed the running car scenario in the closed garage or consuming a poisonous mushroom that we foraged. We debated just about all kinds of ways to do it. But the one that we both liked the most was a trip to the Grand Canyon. There, by the great vistas. He and I as adventurous as we were, it wouldn't be suspicious. We thought that it would look like an accident. During an exploration from the main path. We got too close to the edge and looked over. Then a slippery rock, and skid marks. Our skulls finding the hard rocks. Goodbye.

Grand Canyon became a code between Ray and I. It represented freedom from pain. A place where we could leave it all behind. When we felt frustrated by our physical suffering and overwhelmed by life, we could speak of it in front of others, even. All we needed to say was 'A trip to the Grand Canyon' to communicate to each other that our level of endurance had been reached.

We promised one another that if it got to that point, we would be there together at Grand Canyon. Together.

I'm not sure how serious I was about it. I thought of it. But more so, I wanted to have that with Ray. Part of me was holding onto that promise like a leash, so Ray would not go there alone. Especially after his L.A. surgery when he learned that things were not going to be the same.

It was hard to see him now that he lived in California, but we talked at least once a week. I had to reduce my enthusiasm during our conversations. I was still very empathetic to his discomfort. My surgery was a fabulous success. They replaced my entire right

shoulder joint. I was starting a new career that was less demanding for my body. I was happy again.

I dared not share all of that with him, but he knew. Ray's condition was not getting any better. sounded worse every time we talked. He was in constant and severe pain. He had tried everything. Even with water treatment and was now taking all his doctor's prescribed medications, the heavy opioids, to help ebb the rush of pure pain.

One day I heard from Ray that the recent X-rays showed that the new rod in his back from the L.A. surgery had started to crack! F*CK!

Soon after that, he stopped returning my calls. Once again, I wasn't sure of my offense. Later, I realized that he broke off our friendship. He just didn't want me to be involved with his trip to the proverbial Grand Canyon. He had to break his promise to me and go there alone.

When Pa-yam called to tell me about Ray's passing, I heard something that I should share here. Before I heard that long static, I barely made out Pa-yam

saying, “my dad ended it, his pain...”, then static. I ran to a spot with a better signal, but I missed it.

After that call, I felt so empty. I hadn’t hurt like that. Not since Neda’s passing a few years earlier, he was like my older brother. I was numb. I did not know how I was going to face that family at the funeral. Not his wife and kids, his sisters! The ones that sent him to that hellhole. That was one of the biggest factors in my decision to miss my best friend’s burial.

I now feel that he extended the ultimate love and friendship to me by stopping communicating with me when he did. I like to believe that he thought he would, or could, influence me and I would join. I wished he had called me before his decision to depart.

The world was a better place when he was on the planet. I’d like to celebrate his attitude toward life and his endurance through all that he saw and touched.

Rest in peace my friend.

Ray's zodiac sign: Libra

Ray's favorite place in the world: Yosemite National Park

Ray's hangout: Billy Gordon's Pub, especially Tuesday's live music night

Ray's passion, besides his family and Nature: Americans with Disabilities Act

His favorite quote: "A project without a deadline is a dream."

His favorite line in a song was by his and my favorite band, Pink Floyd:

"All that you touch and all you see is all your life will ever be."

For those who remember Ray's shortcomings and do not agree with the Sainthood moniker, I'd like to remind everyone of Oscar Wilde's (partial) quote: "… every saint has a past, and every sinner has a future."

I would also like you to consider Maria Teresa Goretti, who was Sainted for Forgiveness. She was Canonized in 1950 by Pope Pius XII. A summary from Wikipedia.

On her deathbed, she forgave her attacker and her murderer, it turned out. She was born in 1890. She died at 11!

"Maria Goretti." *Wikipedia*, Wikimedia Foundation, https://en.wikipedia.org/wiki/Maria_Goretti. Accessed 16 Apr. 2026.

I like to add that Saints are often celebrated for their endurance and perseverance in the face of adversity, serving as powerful examples for those seeking strength and resilience. One such figure is Saint Sebastian, a Roman soldier renowned for his unwavering courage and fortitude even after being shot with arrows. Similarly, Saint Monica is remembered for her remarkable patience and steadfast perseverance, especially during times of great personal hardship.

In Ray we have Forgiveness, endurance, and patience.

59

"Saint Sabastian." *Wikipedia*, Wikimedia Foundation, https://en.wikipedia.org/wiki/Maria_Goretti. Accessed 16 Apr. 2026. https://en.wikipedia.org/wiki/Saint_Sebastian

Epilogue, *The final forgiveness*

As an immigrant with English as my second language, I've often needed help expressing my message clearly in this book. I was fortunate to find three great friends later in life, Sam, Jay and Daniel, who became the guiding hands shaping these pages. They challenged me with rewrites, expansions, and thoughtful assignments, taking on the difficult task of editing my story about Ray. Their dedication and support have been invaluable, and they deserve immense credit for helping bring this book to life.

During the long months of editing the book, I reconnected with Pa-yam. I traveled to meet him. He had grown into a capable man—steady, kind, and sure of himself, with a professional's calm about him. Seeing him after all these years struck something deep in me; I got emotional. I feel that Ray would have been proud.

I told him about the book I had written about his father, and that it was soon to be released. I told him

I had done all I could to guard their privacy. We spoke about the donations from the book and how they would go to a foundation for polio research. He agreed without hesitation.

We talked then about the past. I told him about that first phone call he made to me after the tragedy, how I never heard the whole story. After all these years, the gaps were still there. So, I asked him, gently, if he would tell me the sensitive details of Ray's passing.

Over a few beers and teary eyes on both ends, Pa-yam told me Ray took his life with a gun.

Ray once told me he had bought one. The last time I saw him at his home in California, he showed it to me. That's what men do—show each other the things that matter to them.

Pa-yam then told me, too, how mindful Ray had been about the imminent cleanup. Ray went outside, into the open air, with the trees around him and the sky above, and 'jumped over the edge' right there in his backyard. It was his way.

I don't know what stirred in me after that visit, but something did. I realized I had not forgiven him. Not

for leaving me. Not for taking with him the closest friendship I ever had in this world.

So, I forgave Ray at last.

And I believe his family needs to do the same. Maybe this book will bring them some kind of peace, or at least another way to see the life he lived, how the dark caught up to him toward the end when he lost control.

From now on, spreading a little cosmic cheer will be one of my life goals. I'll do it for Ray and in his name.

If you enjoyed the story and would like to support the future writings, please donate a small amount to this PayPal account: paypal.me/VahidHojreh

It's not the amount that you donate; it's the number of donors that is important. Donations of $20 and above will receive a signed paperback of Uncle Ray Ray.

For the next year, I will donate half of the money, donated to Rotary International (A key partner in the Global Polio Eradication Initiative (GPEI), Rotary International has contributed more than $2.7 billion and countless volunteer hours to the fight to end polio. Its PolioPlus program focuses on fundraising, advocacy, and volunteer recruitment. The Rotary Foundation has earned a four-star rating from Charity Navigator and spends over 90% of funding on programs, in Ray's real name.

I hope to have the second 'Book of Saints', named "Neda", by next year.

ISBN: 979-8-234-06670-1

Made in the USA
Coppell, TX
15 June 2026

81357988R00036

Let's begin the journey of twenty-one encampments as recorded in Numbers 33:3–24

1. Rameses: The Journey to Heaven
2. Succoth: Hope of Resurrection
3. Etham: The Presence of God
4. Pi-HaHiroth: God Makes Way Through the Red Sea
5. Marah: Bitterness Turns into Sweetness
6. Elim: Abundance of God
7. By the Red Sea: Victorious
8. Wilderness of Sin: Manna from Heaven
9. Dophkah: God Knocks
10. Alush: Barren Land Bears Fruit in the Presence of the Lord
11. Rephidim: Water from the Rock
12. Wilderness of Sinai: Ten Commandments
13. Kibroth Hattaavah: Grave of Greed
14. Hazeroth: Humility
15. Rithmah: Rebellion of Israelites
16. Rimmon Perez: Begin and End with God
17. Libnah: Purity
18. Rissah: Jew – Mercy of God
19. Kehelathah: Worship
20. Mount Shepher: Glory of God
21. Haradah: Fear of God

1. Rameses: Journey to Heaven

After 430 years of slavery, God wanted to free the Israelites through Moses. And after so many miracles and battles, the Israelites began their freedom journey in Rameses. In Exodus 6:6b: "People of Israel, 'I am the Lord, and I will bring you out from under the burdens of the Egyptians, and I will deliver you from their bondage, and I will redeem you with an outstretched arm.'" The Israelites began their journey under the cover of night, a powerful symbol that God can transform darkness into light. Their departure marked a divine shift: from bondage to freedom, from idolatry to worship of the one true God. Though uncertainty clouded their first steps, scripture reveals that many embarked with unwavering faith and trust in God's promises. Their story reminds us that even in our darkest moments, God leads us toward light, liberation, and truth.

1. Abrahm – journey of faith

We naturally follow someone who promises success, prosperity, and joy, but when God called Abraham, without even thinking or asking questions, he followed God no matter the cost. Because of his faith, God made a covenant with him, and part of it is known of a surety that "your descendants will be sojourners in a land that is not theirs, and will be slaves there, and they will be oppressed for four hundred years; but I will bring judgment on the nation which they serve, and afterward they shall come out with great possessions" (Genesis 15:13–14). Knowing that his descendants must be slaves and needed to go through burdens under the Egyptians, he chose to depend on God all his life. As God promised, they went through a lot of pain and grief in their trials; they forgot the promise, but Abraham always believed that God would bring His promises into fulfillment, and that is exactly why we see the Israelites traveling to the Promised Land.

Abraham believed all these things would take place, and because of his faith, Abraham became the father of nations.

2. Journey to worship God

The Assyrians captured the Israelites, and during this exile, the northern kingdom of Israel abandoned God, and they fell into all kinds of sin and embraced idolatry. And in this situation, we find a man who is faithful, righteous, and loyal to God. The nation, his family, offered sacrifices to the pagan gods like Beth-el and Dan. God Himself speaks about how bad the people of Nineveh are, and Tobit was living in that wicked nation, but Tobit, who never compromised his faith, was strong, and he remained loyal to God. Year after year, he went to Jerusalem to worship God, no matter the cost.

Tobit 1:5–6a, 10–12:

"All the tribes that joined in apostasy used to sacrifice to the calf Ba'al, and so did the house of Naph'tali my forefather. But I alone went often to Jerusalem for the feasts, as it is ordained for all Israel by an everlasting decree. [. . .] Now when I was carried away captive to Nin'eveh, all my brethren and my relatives ate the food of the Gentiles; but I kept myself from eating it, because I remembered God with all my heart."

3. Journey to purify the church and people

King Artaxerxes gave permission to Ezra to take his people to Jerusalem, and he trusted God that He would give him a safe journey. This is what he says in Ezra 8:22: "For I was ashamed to ask the king for a band of soldiers and horsemen to protect us against the enemy on our way; since we had told the king, 'The hand of our God is for good upon all that seek Him, and the power of His wrath is against all that forsake Him.'" Before they started their journey, they fasted and knelt on their knees for a safe journey, and the hand of the Lord was upon them. God "delivered [them] from the hand of the enemy" and led them to Jerusalem (Ezra 8:31b).

After reaching Jerusalem, he purified the church (Ezra 8:36) and the people (Ezra 10:1).

4. Journey to rebuild the SACRED WALLS

Nehemiah received permission from the Persian king and traveled to Jerusalem to rebuild the sacred walls. During this process, he faced humiliation; even a fox jumping on the wall would breach it (Nehemiah 3:35). Threats and plots to kill him could not stop him, because he wept and prayed and surrendered to the Lord (Nehemiah 1:4). With the help of the Lord and support of the people, he rebuilt the walls of Jerusalem in just fifty-two days. When we do the work of God, He will bring it to fulfillment.

2. Succoth: Hope of Resurrection

They started in Rameses and went to Succoth, which means temporary booths and shelters. This is a reminder for us that our life on earth is temporary. Our focus should be on returning to our heavenly home from where we came. "The dust returns to the earth as it was, and the spirit returns to God who gave it" (Ecclesiastes 12:7).

In the Old Testament, Joseph said to his family, "God will visit you, and you shall carry up my bones from here" (Genesis 50:25). And from Succoth, they carried his remains to the Promised Land; this means when we die, our spirit will be taken to the heavens, which Jesus promised us.

Jesus asked his disciples, "Who do you say I am?"

Peter responded, "You are the true son of the living God."

Jesus immediately replied to Peter, saying, "You will receive the keys to the kingdom of Heaven." There are seven keys that will open the doors of paradise.

In the Gospels, Jesus says to Peter that the keys of the kingdom will be given to him, and there are seven keys that will open the doors of Heaven.

1. Key of repentance

In the gospel of Mathew, Jesus speaks about the people of Nineveh. They will occupy the throne and judge the present generation because the men of Nineveh, after listening to the prophet Jonah, repented and felt sorry for their sins and turned to God. Even though the Nineveh people worshiped false gods and committed all sorts of evil things, because they repented, they received Heaven.

2. Key of discipleship

Peter asked Jesus, "Lord, we have left everything and followed you. What is it of profit for us or reward for us?"

Jesus replied, "At the renewal of all things and when the son of man sits on His glorious throne, you who have followed me will sit on twelve thrones and will judge the twelve tribes of Israel." And further, for all of us, he said, "Whoever has left houses, brothers or sisters, father or mother, wife or children for my sake will receive a hundredfold as much; they will receive eternal life." Whoever takes up discipleship will receive Heaven.

3. Key of faith

Jesus speaks about the queen of the south who will receive a throne and will judge the present generation. The reason God highly praised and appreciated her and granted her a high position is her faith! This woman was not a believer; she was a pagan woman who traveled 1,500 miles to hear the wisdom of Solomon. And, after hearing Solomon, she said, "If a man of this world is so wise, how much wiser is the God who created him?" She admired the wisdom of God and became a strong believer. That is why God gives her a throne in Heaven. Mathew 12:42a: "The queen of the South will arise at the judgment with this generation and condemn it; for she came from the ends of the earth to hear the wisdom of Solomon."

4. Key of righteousness

From the moment St. Paul became a follower of Christ, he remained faithful till the end of his life. He made sure that he fought the good fight, kept the faith, and in all his humiliation, he finished the race with confidence and trust in the Lord. He said, "I am waiting for my reward of eternal life in faith; the Lord will crown me for the righteous life that I lived till the last breath of my life."

2 Timothy 4:7–8: "I have fought the good fight, I have finished the race, I have kept the faith. Henceforth there is laid up for me

the crown of righteousness, which the Lord, the righteous judge, will award to me on that Day, and not only to me but also to all who have loved His appearing."

5. Key of good deeds

On the feast day of Pentecost, which is the sacred festival of the seven weeks, the Tobit family prepared a delicious meal, and, sitting before the abundance of food, he said to his son, "Go and bring a poor man of our brethren. You may find them among the exiles in Nineveh, who has fear of the Lord, so that he can eat with us. We will wait until he comes."

When his son returned, he said to him, "One of our own people has been murdered and thrown in the marketplace, and now he lies there strangled."

After hearing this, Tobit was shocked, and he immediately jumped and went to bury that person, and then he came home and ate his food in sorrow. All of Tobith's life, he had done acts of mercy and charity. That is why Jesus said in Mathew 16:27, "For the Son of man is to come with his angels in the glory of his Father, and then he will repay every man for what he has done." Spiritual and corporal works of mercy and good deeds are the key to Heaven.

6. Key of fear of the Lord

God asked Jeremiah to invite the Rechabites into the temple and requested that they take wine. Without even thinking, they said, "We will not touch it." They loved their ancestors, their commands, and their customs. One of the commands of their ancestor Jonadab was to live a normal life, which meant keep yourself away from drinking, building houses, planting vineyards, but rather live humbly. "Because you have obeyed the command of Jon'adab your father, and kept all his precepts, and done all that he commanded you, therefore thus says the Lord of hosts, the God of Israel: Jon'adab the son of Rechab shall never lack a man to stand before me" (Jeremiah 35:18–19).

Malachi 3:16–17: "Then those who feared the Lord spoke with one another; the Lord heeded and heard them, and a book of remembrance was written before Him of those who feared the Lord and thought on His name. 'They shall be mine,' says the Lord of hosts, 'my special possession on the day when I act, and I will spare them as a man spares his son who serves him.'" Fear of the Lord will always get us to Heaven.

7. Key of Sabbath

God created the world in six days, and on the seventh (that is Sabbath), He rested. He blessed the Sabbath day and made it holy, and later he made it one of the commandments. In the book of Isaiah, we find a foreigner who loved the Sabbath day and kept it holy all his life. God promised him that He would bring him to the holy mountain and give them joy in His Zion (Isaiah 56:6–7). When you keep His commandments, Christ is with you wherever you go (Joshua 1:7–8).

3. Etham: The Presence of God

1. Presence of God

From Succoth, they went to Etham. In Etham, the presence of the Lord came in the form of a cloud and a pillar of fire, and He accompanied the Israelites. Moses spent a lot of his time with God. Knowing the value of His presence, he said to the Lord, "I need your presence. I will not go without you." And the Lord agreed to escort them. Moses always looked to God for His guidance and direction in all he did. That is why God led him.

2. Presence of God: Miracles

Jesus appointed seventy-two disciples, and He sent them two by two into every town and place where He was about to visit. Before sending them, He said, "I am sending you like lambs in the midst of the wolves. However, carry no bag, no purse, no sandals, and salute and completely depended on God." They went in complete trust, and after completing the mission, they returned with joy. While they were giving reports of their journey, they said "Lord, in your name we have done miracles, wonders, and even demons are subject to us in your name." The Lord said, "I saw Satan fall like lightning from Heaven." Additionally, the Lord said to them, "Behold, I give you authority to tread upon serpents, scorpions, and over all the power of the enemy. Nothing shall hurt you! Nevertheless, don't rejoice over those but rejoice because your names are written in the book of life." When God's presence comes with us, we can do wonders, and above all, our names will be written in the book of life.

3. Presence of God: Protection

Jesus was in constant communication with God the Father in prayer. After the feeding of the five thousand, he said to his disciples to get into the boat and go to the other side of Bethsaida. He went up the mountain to pray. While Jesus was praying, he saw his disciples struggling from afar; they were fighting against a storm on the sea. They were scared and distressed, the waves were very violent, and immediately Jesus came walking on the water and calmed the sea and saved them. God sees everything. We are always in His sight, and He will protect and save us.

4. Presence of God: Worth Pursuing

Every human soul longs to be filled with something, but nothing in this world can satisfy that longing except the presence of God. David writes in his Psalm, "As the deer longs for water, my soul longs for my God" (42:1). In Song of Solomon 3:1, we see the bride seeking her beloved. "Upon my bed by night I sought Him whom my soul loves; I sought Him, but found Him not; I called Him, but He gave no answer." The bride went and searched for Him, and after searching, she found Him, held Him, and would not let Him go. That is what we read in Jeremiah 29:13: "You will seek me and find me; when you seek me with all your heart." When we find the "Groom," everything will change in our lives for the better. Our cup of joy will overflow.

4. Pi-HaHiroth: God Makes a Way

The Israelites came to Pi-HaHiroth and stood by the Red Sea.

1. Holy Spirit makes a way

From Rameses to Pi-HaHiroth, the journey was uneventful. The Israelites thought they were free from any threat, and it looked as if they would reach the Promised Land safely. They thought that they had evaded their enemies, but they were close by. The Egyptians did not want the Israelites to escape, so they continued to pursue them; they would catch up at the Red Sea. The Israelites were approaching a dead end, trapped between the enemy and the sea.

It seemed as if the Red Sea was waiting to devour them. If they continued, they would sink and die in the sea. But if they stopped, the Egyptians would capture or kill them as they were closing in with chariots and horses behind them. They thought there was no way out, and this was the end of their journey to the Promised Land and maybe even an end to their life.

If we have faith in God, He will surprise us. He will perform miracles and bring about wonders in our lives beyond our imagination. God spoke to Moses and said, "Take your staff and strike the Red Sea!" He did as instructed, and the sea was split in two, creating a path for the Israelites to escape. The sea floor was dry, and the water stood like walls on both sides. As they continued through the sea, God performed another miracle. In the middle of the night, God gave the Israelites light to guide them safely through, while darkness fell on the Egyptians to keep them from reaching the Israelites. The Holy Spirit, through a pillar of fire, brought light to the path of the Israelites. He did not take them by wind or around, but through the Red Sea.

2. Jesus makes a way

While Joseph and Mary were in Bethlehem shortly after the birth of Jesus, an angel of the Lord appeared to Joseph and said, "Take the child and his mother and flee to Egypt and remain there until I tell you." King Herod was about to begin what is known as "the slaughter of the innocents" (The execution of all male children under two years old) for fear of losing his power to Jesus. Joseph immediately, without any delay, took Jesus and his mother by night and began the journey to Egypt (Mathew 2:13).

Just imagine traveling 400 miles from Bethlehem to Egypt. They needed to travel by night so as not to be seen by anyone who could report back to Herod. In the middle of the night, with a newborn child on foot, with only a donkey to help, traveling through forests and mountains, in a desert with no proper route or direction. There were all sorts of dangers around them as they traveled.

Nothing affected them; no wild animal, no thief, no darkness stopped them because Jesus, the light of the world, made way for them and protected them in their journey. Three days of traveling in the middle of the night and in the midst of all sorts of danger. It was not easy, but their trust in the Lord paved the way for them.

3. God makes a way

Jacob went to Laban and faithfully served him for many years, and Laban loved him. Once he even mentioned, "If you will allow me to say so, I have learned by divination that the Lord has blessed me because of you" (Genesis 30:27). After a few years, Laban started to hate Jacob, and as the days continued, that hate grew stronger, and he did not pay him fair wages.

One day, Jacob told his wife Rebekah, "When I came here, I found your father's favor, but now I no longer find such favor with your father."

Jacob, with the help of the Lord, took his wives, children, and flocks, and in the night, he quietly left for his homeland. Laban pursued him with anger, and God appeared to him in a dream and said, "Take heed that you say not a word to Jacob, either good or bad" (Genesis 31:24b). He reached home safely with his family because the Lord went with him and made a clear path. When God is with you, nothing can stand in your way, and in Isaiah, we read, "I will go before you and level the mountains" (Isaiah 45:2).

5. Marah

1. Marah: bitterness into sweetness

From Pi-HaHiroth, they went to Marah. After a long journey, the Israelites came to Marah, and they were exhausted and very thirsty. But the water in Marah was bitter and undrinkable. Moses takes a branch and tosses it into the water, and immediately the bitter water turns into a sweet, very drinkable water. Since Moses obeyed God, a miracle happened. Similarly, when we obey God in all situations, the bitterness in our lives will turn into sweetness.

2. When you think it's all over . . . GOD begins

Jesus, along with His disciples and His mother Mary, was invited to a wedding feast in Cana. Everything was going well, and everyone was joyful at the wedding. Long before the wedding was supposed to end, they ran out of wine. The proprietor of the wedding thought the wedding feast would end when the people came to know that there was no more wine. He was sure that this would bring shame, disappointment, and embarrassment to the family of the bride and groom.

But through the intercession of Mother Mary, God intervened, and Jesus told the servants to go and fill the jars to the brim with water. They did as Jesus instructed, and He turned the water into the best wine they had ever tasted. Sometimes we may have shame, disappointment, and embarrassment in our lives, and we aren't sure how we can go on. It's always good for us to go to our heavenly Mother for her intercession. God will remove the emptiness and bitterness in our lives. So don't think it's all over; have faith and believe that God will begin a new chapter in your life.

Two things:

1. When you think it's all over, go to our Mother.
2. Regardless of how bad a sinner you think you are, God can turn dirty water into sweet wine; He can take anyone and turn them into a saint!

3. Sinner into Saint

The Samaritan woman came to the well during the afternoon. She was completely burdened. She had a past "Jar" that was filled with all sorts of shame and humiliation. Knowing all these things, Jesus was waiting at the well to save her. She came to the well all by herself, and Jesus asked her for water, and He slowly revealed her sins to her. He said, "The present man you are living with is not your husband." During this conversation, she realized that Jesus was the Messiah. He spoke to her with mercy and compassion, and He offered her the living water.

The jar that she was carrying symbolized her past life, and that is why she left it at the well. She said to herself, "Because of this jar, I am sinning. I'm having multiple affairs, and I'm using it for my sinful life. I don't need this jar anymore now that I have found the living water." From that moment, she was transformed, and her entire village was also transformed by her witness.

When you are able to let go of what is making you commit sin, God will make you a saint!

6. Elim: Twelve Springs of Water and Seventy Palm Trees - Abundance of God

Blessings of God

The Israelites traveled from Marah and went to Elim, which has seventy palm trees and twelve springs of water. In the wilderness, God provided them with rest and an abundance of blessings. He bestows many blessings on us, more than we deserve, and when He does, no person or circumstance can stop Him.

There are five ways that God blesses us:

1. When you put God first – blessings flow

The Israelites returned from exile, they listened to Zechariah, and they placed God first above everything. They had lost all that they had and were beginning to experience the blessings of God in abundance. Their fields were producing a good harvest, their livestock multiplied each day, and their households were flourishing. This is what we are told in Proverbs 10:22: "The blessing of the Lord makes rich, and He adds no sorrow with it." The blessings from God were beyond measure, which made them vulnerable to thieves. Therefore, God himself became a wall of fire and protected them from all corners. They lived in peace because God became the protector of their families and wealth.

2. Obedience of God – blessings flow

God blessed Abraham and promised that He would bless his descendants. Isaac trusted and obeyed God as his father Abraham did. A severe famine came during the time of Isaac, and he wanted to flee Egypt in hopes of saving his family. But God asked him to remain. Isaac didn't see any possibility of survival, but in trusting God and in obedience to Him, he remained. Isaac was poor and had very few means to care for and feed his family. He sowed the seeds he had, and Isaac reaped a hundredfold in that same year because of his obedience to God (Genesis 26:12). This obedience made Isaac a very rich and prosperous man (Genesis 26:13). The Philistines envied him, but no enemy or opposition could stop the blessings he received from God. When we place all our trust in God and obey His commands, we will also reap a hundredfold and be prosperous.

3. Engage in God's work – blessings flow

The Israelites returned from exile and were busy building houses and planting a harvest. They were trying to build a better life, and they were content for nearly sixteen years. During this time, they neglected God and the temple! Their efforts brought very little. They sowed and expected a great harvest, but they got very little. They were focused on their needs and not on God. They neglected the house of the Lord, and it was in ruins, and that is why Haggai warned them.

"You have sown much, and harvested little; you eat, but you never have enough; you drink, but you never have your fill; you clothe yourselves, but no one is warm; and he who earns wages earns wages to put them into a bag with holes" (Haggai 1:6).

They were only concerned with their needs and were not giving God His due. They realized this after they lost favor with God and through the words of the prophet. They understood that they had made a mistake and repented. From that day forward, God blessed them. He said, "From this day I will bless you. Let us place God's work, His temple, mission, and kingdom, above every work; we will have blessings from God in abundance."

"But seek first his kingdom and his righteousness, and all these things shall be yours as well" (Matthew 6:33).

4. Turn your house into a prayer – blessings flow

King David was transporting the covenant of the Lord, and Uzzah reached out to steady the Ark of the Covenant, but God struck him for touching it. King David got frightened and placed it in the house of Obed Edom. The moment the covenant of the Lord came to his house, he turned it into a house of prayer and worship. Because of his reverence, God blessed him abundantly. King David recalls the Ark of the Covenant and tells his servants to go and find out what happened to Obed Edom, and they report to the king, saying he is blessed by God.

When our home becomes a house of prayer and worship, God will bring many blessings into it.

5. Generosity – blessings flow

When we give of our time, treasure, and talents to God and our neighbors, especially the most vulnerable, through our generosity, God will open the heavens and pour out His blessings for us.

"Bring the full tithes into the storehouse, that there may be food in my house; and thereby put me to the test, says the Lord of hosts, if I will not open the windows of heaven for you and pour down for you an overflowing blessing" (Malachi 3:10).

7. Celebration: Crossing the Red Sea

1. When God leads – nothing can stop Him

With the mighty hand of God, the Israelites were able to cross the Red Sea. They celebrated this victory with dancing and singing; their joy had no limits. God was with them; He used His mighty hand and performed miracles in order for the Israelites to be set free. With His outstretched arm, He made it possible for them to cross the sea. When God stands for us and we are able to follow the path He has set before us, no enemy, no obstacle, nothing will stop God from His divine intervention. The Israelites had seen all of these wonders with their own eyes, and they praised Him. They sang, "*The Lord is my strength and my song, and He has become my salvation*" (Exodus 15:2a).

2. When God is with you – nothing can stop you

King David set his journey toward Jerusalem. The Jebusites underestimated the power of David and the power of his God. They laughed and mocked him, saying, "*You will not get in here; even the blind and the lame can ward you off.*" In other words, they were trying to tell him to go home, to save his dignity, because they thought men were incapable of conquering Jerusalem.

David entered in the name of the Lord and captured it for Him. He declared it as the capital city of God. After the victory, David brought the presence of God to Jerusalem, and it became the place of worship for generations. Mockery turned into music; humiliation turned into hallelujahs. They continued singing from generation to generation!

"Rejoice in the Lord always; again I will say, Rejoice" (Philippians 4:4).

3. When God wills – nothing can stop Him

The crippled man seeking alms at the gate of the temple was carried to the temple every day by his family. He was never allowed into the temple because he was a crippled man. In Jewish tradition, there is a saying, **"No crippled man can enter the temple."** The crippled man's heart longed for God; everything about him was perfect, except for his legs. He thought he would never be able to enter the temple of God.

He looked at Peter and John and asked for alms; he was expecting them to give him a few coins. But Peter looked at this tired and broken man and said, "I don't have silver and gold, but I have the name of Jesus, and in the name of Jesus Christ, I command you to get up and walk." Immediately, he got up and went straight to the temple and praised God. He not only received healing, but also entry into the temple of God. When God wills your entry, nothing can stop it.

8. Wilderness of Sin: Manna from Heaven

1. Depend on God every day for providence

During the Israelites' travels, they witnessed the wonders of the Lord. God guided them through the vast and dangerous lands with their wild animals and rough terrain. For most of their journey, the land was dry and waterless. He brought forth water from the flinty rock, and they were guarded by the angels of God (Deuteronomy 8:15). Through all of these miracles, they were unchanged and became indignant. Instead of thanking God, the Israelites were grumbling and complaining about their journey. God was gracious to them and gave them manna from Heaven. He gave them enough for each day, meaning that they should know that God would provide for them every day. In the Our Father prayer, we pray, "Lord, give us our daily bread." God will provide for us daily! *"Give me neither poverty nor riches; feed me with the food that is needful for me"* (Proverbs 30:8b).

2. Depend on God till the end

God did wonders in the life of King Asa. Asa did what was right in the sight of the Lord. He removed idols and encouraged others to trust in God. Asa was given victory over the Ethiopians for being a faithful servant. But in the end, he failed to depend on God.

a. King Basha of Israel waged war against Asa King of Judah. Asa, who did what was right in the sight of God, failed to depend on God. He did not consult with God or depend on Him. Rather, he subjected himself to Ben Hadad, the King of Aram, and allied with gold and silver.

b. Asa, the king of Judah, had foot disease, and in his sickness, he turned away from God. He turned to sorcery and died from his illness. If we depend on God till the end, we will not end up like Asa, the king of Judah.

3. Depend on God for protection

The Israelites were in great trouble, and Haman, a high-ranking official in the Persian Empire influenced by the king, passed a decree to annihilate all the Jews in Persia. Knowing this plot, Mordecai intervened and warned Queen Esther.

"Think not that in the king's palace you will escape any more than all the other Jews. For if you keep silence at such a time as this, relief and deliverance will rise for the Jews from another quarter, but you and your father's house will perish. And who knows whether you have not attained royalty for such a time as this?" (Esther 4:13b–14).

Queen Esther knew if she approached the king without his permission, she would be put to death. "If I approach him, he will put me to death." Depending on God, she says, "If I die, I die, if I perish, I perish but let me do it for the people of God." She sent word to Mordecai. "Fast for me three days without eating and drinking. My servants and I will do the same." She trusted and depended on God. Queen Esther approached the king, and God exposed Haman's plot, and He saved all the Israelites. When we trust and depend on God, He will always save us.

9. Dophkah: God Knocks

The Israelites reached a place called Dophkah, which means God knocks.

1. When God knocks, stay in His presence

Mephibosheth lost his father, Jonathan, and his grandfather, King Saul. He was quickly pushed aside and forgotten. And to add to all of his misery, at the age of five, he was crippled after his nurse dropped him while fleeing when news came of Saul and Jonathan's deaths. Mephibosheth did not question God or blame his nurse. He didn't seek revenge; rather, he placed his trust in God and waited patiently. King David remembered the promise he had made to Jonathan, his friend, and wanted to repay his kindness. King David sent messengers to see if anyone was left from Jonathan's family. He was told that there was one crippled man, and he was the son of Jonathan. David said, "Go and bring him to me."

Mephibosheth came to the king and bowed down in fear. He said humbly, "Your servant, what is it that you should notice a dead dog like me?"

But David said, "From now on, you will sit at my table and will eat with me." When God knocks, He gives us honor and desires for us to sit in His presence forever.

2. God knocks so He can speak to us

The people of Judah and Jerusalem gathered in the presence of God and prayed to the Lord in hopes of being saved. While they were fasting and praying, the spirit of the Lord came upon a man named Jahaziel. From all the people gathered, he was chosen by God to speak. Filled with courage and boldness, he said, "Have faith and trust the Lord. This battle is not ours; it is God's." He filled their hearts with faith and trust, and God defeated their enemy.

God picks us to declare His will and His mighty deeds. Remain faithful and always be ready to do His will.

3. God knocks to give fulfillment

Jacob betrayed his father and brother. He secretly ran away to his uncle's house to save his life. He was regretful, and he had many questions about his future. After a long journey in the wilderness, he took a stone as a pillow and slept. God gently spoke to him in a dream. He did not frighten him, but God showed him his future. And in that dream, Jacob had a vision of a ladder connecting Heaven and earth. Angels were traveling up and down, and God was standing at the top of the ladder. He made a promise to Jacob, saying,

"I am with you. I will keep you. I will bring you back. I will not leave you until I have done what I promised." That changed everything for Jacob. Trust in God's promises, and He will bring them into fulfillment. Even though we are unfaithful and betray God daily, God is always faithful to His promises.

10. Alush: Barren Land

The Israelites traveled and came to a place called Alush. God sustains even in a barren land.

For God, nothing is impossible, and when we surrender ourselves and place ourselves in the presence of the Lord, He will always sustain his people. In the wilderness, in mountains, and even in barren land, His sustenance continues.

1. Dry staff bears fruit in the presence of the Lord

The Israelites (God's chosen people) were always fighting against God. And now they were fighting among themselves for authority and leadership. God summoned all the tribes of Israel to bring a dry staff. Twelve leaders brought a dry staff to Moses. He asked them to place the staffs in the presence of the Lord. They did as Moses commanded them to. They closed all the doors and went on their way. In the morning, when Moses came to the presence of the Lord, Aaron's staff had sprouted and produced almonds; all the other staffs remained the same. All this happened in one night; a lifeless piece of wood became alive and fruitful (Numbers 17:8). Even though they were in a dry, barren land, since they surrendered themselves in the presence of God, He sustained them! This is what happens when we place ourselves and our problems in His presence. God will continuously make us fruitful and will turn our sorrows into joy.

2. Hezekiah placed a letter of mockery in the presence of the Lord

King Sennacherib sent a letter to King Hezekiah and said, "Let not your God deceive you, and remember no one can save you or Jerusalem from King Assyria." Assyria was very powerful, and it conquered countless kingdoms and left behind a great deal of destruction. To frighten them, King Sennacherib named the list of nations and kings that they destroyed:

"Have the gods of the nations delivered them, the nations which my fathers destroyed, Gozan, Haran, Rezeph, and the people of Eden who were in Tel-assar? Where is the king of Hamath, the king of Arpad, the king of the city of Sepharva'im, the king of Hena, or the king of Ivvah?" (2 Kings 19:12–13)

King Hezekiah received the letter and went up the mountain and prayed. He said, "The Assyrians have destroyed nations and have cast their gods into the fire, for they were not gods but made of human hands, wood and stone; therefore, they were destroyed. Lord, you are the true God, and there is no other god like you, and you cannot be mocked." God sent an angel and defeated King Sennacherib's army, and he went home defeated. While Sennacherib was in Nineveh worshipping his god, in the house of Nisroch, his sons killed him. When you place yourself in His presence, God of the living will bring you victory as He brought victory to Hezekiah.

3. Leah put God first, and God glorified her

Leah loved her husband more than she loved her parents, her life, and even more than her God. Because of this, she was overlooked, unloved, and even rejected by her husband. Her life was miserable the moment she placed her husband above everyone and everything.

After having her first son, Reuben, she said, "Now my husband will love me." But he never loved her. After having her second son, Simeon, she said, "God gave this child to me because my husband has no love for me." After having her third son, Levi, she said, "Now my husband will be attached to me." But that never happened. Leah realized that she made a big mistake by placing her husband above everything and everyone. So, she turned to God and placed Him above everything. After having her fourth son, Judah, she said, "From today I will praise the Lord." The moment she placed God above everything, He glorified her from generation to generation. Jesus came from the lion of Judah. Place God above everything and everyone, and He will glorify you!

11. Rephidim: Water from the Rock

1. Rock – Water

The Israelites traveled to Rephidim from Alush. They were thirsty and were complaining to Moses, saying, "Have you brought us out of Egypt to kill us, our children, and cattle out of thirst?" Moses cried out to the Lord and said, "What shall I do with these people? They are ready to stone me."

God said to Moses, "Take the elders of Israel with you and strike the rock," and he did as God commanded him, and water came gushing out of the rock. They were in the desert, and there was no water in sight, but God brought water from the rock. For God, anything is possible.

During the time of the prophet Elisha, the king of Israel, the king of Judah, and the king of Edom went on a march for seven days to the Moabites. There was no water for their armies or the cattle that followed them. Elisha said to them, "Even though there is no wind or rain, these valleys will be filled with water." The next morning, about the time of the offering, waters filled the valley, and they had the water needed for themselves and their cattle, and they were able to conquer the Moabites. For God, anything is possible.

2. The Rock – God's Kingdom

Rock represents the kingdom of God, and Jesus states this in Mathew 16:18b: "on this rock I will build my church, and the powers of death shall not prevail against it." Many kingdoms have come and shone for a while and disappeared permanently, but the kingdom of God remains forever.

The Egyptian kingdom ruled for a while and disappeared permanently. The Assyrian kingdom, the Babylonian Empire, The Medo-Persian Empire, the Greek Empire, and the Roman Empire: all of these kingdoms ruled for a while and then disappeared permanently. They reigned powerfully with force, but eventually they all fell and faded away. The Kingdom of God will never fade away. God has reigned and will continue reign with love and mercy forever.

God's kingdom will remain forever.

3. God's promise remains forever

God is faithful to His promise, and David knew this truth well. David told his son Solomon to be strong and courageous. He said, "Fear not, be not dismayed; for the Lord God, even my God, is with you. He will not fail you or forsake you, until all the work for the service of the house of the Lord is finished" (1 Chronicles 28:20).

These are not words; they are promises and a declaration of God's faithfulness. From the moment Prophet Samuel anointed him, God was with him, and He fulfilled all the promises that were made to David. As God promised, He remained with Solomon until he completed the temple. What God starts, He finishes! God will remain faithful and keep His promises until the end.

4. The name of Jesus remains forever

A new king arose over Egypt, and he did not know who Joseph was. Joseph, at one time, was a powerful governor in Egypt, and he did many great things. He saved his people from a famine, and his name was spread across the entire region. How could such a great, powerful man be forgotten? All the power in the world will be forgotten one day. All the names, fortune, and fame will fade away. All the powerful kings, even the greatest in history, will be forgotten. But there is one King, one name, who will never be forgotten. Jesus Christ, His name is above all names, and He will reign forever and ever, Amen.

12. Mount Sinai: Ten Commandments

1. Ten Commandments – success

Moses loved going up the mountain to pray. He climbed the mountain many times to seek God. The Israelites left Rephidim and went to the wilderness of Sinai. Moses told the people to be holy, and he consecrated them, and they washed their garments. On the morning of the third day, there was thunder, lightning, and thick clouds upon the mountain. A very loud trumpet blast, and all the people trembled. Everyone stood at the foot of the mountain, and it was wrapped in smoke. The mountain quaked, and God descended upon it as fire. Moses took Aaron and went up the mountain, and God gave him the Ten Commandments. Later, God told Joshua that the key to success is not military power but the Ten Commandments (Joshua 1:7–9). God gave him the three principles of the Ten Commandments:

1. Follow all the commandments which my servant Moses commanded you, and you will have success wherever you go.

2. Meditate on the Ten Commandments day and night, and you will be prosperous.

3. Do everything that is written in it, and God will be with you wherever you go.

Obey His commandments, and you will also inherit these principles.

2. Ten Commandments – honor

God gives honor to those who follow His Commandments. In the book of Isaiah, God said to the Eunuchs, "Don't call yourself a dry tree. Since you have followed my Sabbath faithfully, and kept my covenant, I will give them, in my house and within my walls:

a. A monument.

b. A name better than sons and daughters and an everlasting name which shall not be cut off (Isaiah 56:3–5).

3. When you mock God's word – death

God spoke to Jeremiah faithfully, and he did what the Lord commanded him. With the help of Baruch, his scribe, he faithfully wrote down God's word on a scroll. The words of warnings, repentance, and acts of mercy, he brought before King Jehoiakim. Instead of embracing what was written and following God's commands, he showed no signs of repentance. Rather, he took a knife, cut the scroll into pieces, and threw it into the fire. Jehoiakim burned God's message.

Because he burned the word, God declared a harsh punishment upon him.

He shall have no one to sit upon the throne of David. And his dead body shall be cast out into the heat by day and frost by night (Jeremiah 36:30).

13. Kibroth Hattaavah: Grave of Greed

1. Greed – sickness

They saw the glory of God on Mount Sinai, and they received His Commandments. After seeing such splendor, they left for Kibroth Hattaavah. Throughout their journey, God has gave them manna. God said, "Gather only what is needed for the day." But they gathered extra, and since they did not obey God or have faith in Him, all that they gathered became infested with maggots and began to smell; it was rotten. If you don't have faith and trust in God, even the things He has blessed you with will begin to sour and rot.

Even though they did not obey God, He showed them mercy. He provided them nourishment every day as He promised. They grew tired of the manna and were not satisfied with the blessings God provided. They were constantly complaining! They began complaining again in Kibroth Hattaavah, saying, "In Egypt we ate fish without cost, cucumbers, lemons, the leeks, the onions, the garlic, but now we are famished; we have nothing to look forward to but this manna."

Moses cried out to the Lord, saying, "Why are you burdening me with these people? They are constantly complaining about not having meat. Where can I get meat for all these people? Lord, I am not able to bear these people any longer. Better that you take my life so that I no longer have to face them."

They complained about their enemies, and He led them through red sea and saved them. They complained about water, so God gave them water from the rock. They complained about being hungry, and God gave them manna from Heaven to eat. And now they were complaining about not having meat for food.

Once again, God had compassion and gave them quail in abundance. This is the mercy of God.

Our actions will always have consequences, though. While the meat was in their mouth and they were about to chew it, the anger of the Lord burned against the people. He struck them with a severe plague. In this place, they craved for more, and it became a burial ground. That is why Kibroth Hattaavah means graves of craving (Numbers 11:13). God teaches us not to be greedy but rather be generous.

2. Generosity – access to God

King David was constantly blessed, and at the same time, he had countless issues. He had trouble with King Saul, he had trouble with his counselor Ahithophel, he had trouble with his enemies, and he was having issues with his own son Absalom. Most of the people abandoned King David and joined his son. He had to escape his own kingdom to save his life.

David and his men were tired, weary, and heartbroken. They had nothing to eat in the wilderness of Mahanaim, and they were in despair. Barzillai, a wealthy man from Gilead, came to their aid with provisions. He gave them beds, covers, basins, pottery, wheat, barley flour, roasted grain, beans, lentils, honey, butter, and cheese from the flocks and herds. David and his men were able to eat.

Slowly, things changed, and their situation became better. David was restored as a king once again, and he remembered the kindness of Barzillai. He invited him to be with him in his palace and to eat at his table for the rest of his life. Barzillai responded by saying, "My Lord, thank you for this honor, and I will be very grateful to you for this kind invitation. But I am eighty years old, and I would like to die in my place. May I request that you give that honor and kindness to my son?" David granted his request and confirmed his promise to Barzillai, saying, "Your son, Chimham, will come with me, and I will do for him whatever you wish."

Generosity gives us access to God and gives our lineage access to God, which lasts forever.

3. Generosity – honor

Another instance when David was having complications: The servant of Mephibosheth, Zeba, the son of Jonathan, came to help him and his men when they were in desperate need.

He brought provisions, and the king asked, "'Why have you brought these?'

"Ziba answered, 'The [donkeys] are for the king's household to ride on, the bread and summer fruit for the young men to eat, and the wine for those who faint in the wilderness to drink'" (2 Samuel 16:2).

"Since you showed kindness and loyalty, whatever belongs to Mephibosheth belongs to you." kindness gave him honor. He was once a slave, but his kindness made him a master.

Kindness always brings us honor.

14. Hazeroth: Pride

1. Pride – sickness

Moses, Aaron, and Miriam were Saintly people. They lived their life doing God's Work. The people always looked to Moses for answers when they had issues. God was doing great things through Moses, and the people were resentful of his good work.

Instead of being humble and accepting God's plan, internally, they were jealous and were murmuring, "Why not us! Lord, what about us! Don't we deserve what our brother has? It's not fair that we, too, deserve honor and attention." The resentment was growing deeper and deeper, and one day they said, "Why has God not spoken to us?"

We see how pride was taking over them. They longed for attention, recognition, and expected God to give them more. They were not satisfied or content with the blessings God had given them. They longed for more authority and control. This is why they spoke out of pride and said, "Does God only speak through Moses?"

Moses remained humble and calm through all the resentment, and it was best that he did. God stepped in and spoke. He summoned three of them to the tent and said, "With prophets I speak in dreams and visions, but with Moses I speak face to face." Since they spoke against Moses, God struck Miriam with leprosy. He did this not to punish them but to humble them. God corrects those who he loves. Moses prayed to God, and He healed Miriam. Remember Jesus' words when He said, "Those who exalt themselves will be humbled, and those who humble themselves will be exalted."

2. Humility – throne

From the time Samson was elected king, Saul battled and longed for power and the throne. At the end of King David's reign, the people were discussing among themselves who would be the successor to the king after he died. Adonijah wanted the throne; he wanted to be the next king. So, he bought chariots and horses and got fifty men to run before him. He had sheep, oxen, and fatlings slaughtered. Adonijah had a banquet for all the king's sons and all the royal officials. And people sang, "Hail the king, hail the king," and he exalted himself. But he did not have the approval of his father or of God. Solomon, the son of King David, saw all these things but remained silent. He did not blame his mother or his father, nor did he question God. Rather, he said to himself, "May God's will be done."

With the instructions of the Prophet Nathan, Bathsheba, the mother of Solomon, went to King David and said, "You promised your handmaid that your son Solomon would be the next king and would sit on the throne after you. But now Adonijah has declared himself the king."

The king promised her again and said, "Your son will be the king, and he will sit upon my throne in my palace."

King David summoned Zadok the priest, Nathan the prophet, and Benaiah's son of Jehoiada and told them, "Take with you the royal officials and mount my son Solomon upon my mule." With the instructions of King David, Zadok the priest took the horn of oil from the tabernacle and anointed him as king of Israel. They blew the ram's horn, and all the people shouted, "Long live King Solomon."

Adonijah exalted himself and was humbled by God.

King Solomon humbled himself and was exalted by God.

3. Humility – authority

In the book of Isaiah, we hear about a manager of the royal household (Shebna). He built a tomb for himself on the hillside. He was doing everything in his power to make a name for himself. He wanted fame, and he was proud of his position and his belongings.

Isaiah questioned him and said, "Who do you think you are? What right do you have to carve a tomb for yourself? I will pick you up like a ball and toss you out. You are a disgrace to your master. The Lord will bring you down, and you will die beside your chariots, which you are so proud of."

a. God threw away Shebna and placed Eliakim, son of Hilkiah, in his place.

b. He took the robe, the belt, and the authority of Shebna and gave them all to Eliakim.

c. God gave complete authority to Eliakim (under the king, the descendants of David).

d. He will have the keys; what he opens no one will close, what he closes, no one will open. He will be a great honor to his family.

Always remember! What God gives, He can also take away. Therefore, always remain humble.

15. Rithmah: Rebellion

The Israelites rebelled against God, yet even in their disobedience God's mercy was available to them.

1. Rebellion – the loss of paradise

Moses sent twelve men to the wilderness of Paran. He sent them to scope out the Canaan land for forty days. On the forty-first day, they brought a report of their findings. In scriptural history, people experienced the power of God on the forty-first day.

On the forty-first day – good news

Noah experienced rain and darkness for forty days, and on the forty-first day there was light. Moses went to the mountain of the Lord for forty days, and on the forty-first day, he brought the Ten Commandments. Twelve men went to scout the Canaan land for forty days, and on the forty-first day, two out of the twelve returned with good news. The Israelites traveled for forty years, and in the forty-first year, they possessed the Promised Land. Jesus fasted for forty days in the wilderness, and on the forty-first day, Satan disappeared. After the resurrection of Christ, Jesus appeared to his disciples on the fortieth day, and on the forty-first day, He ascended into Heaven. Remember, there will always be a forty-first day. God's promises will be fulfilled!

Rebellion – the loss of paradise

Twelve men returned from Canaan and brought with them the first fruits of the land. They said that the land was flowing with milk and honey. The land was good, but the people were strong, and the cities were fortified and very large. The people of Israel cried out to the Lord and said, "We should have died in Egypt or in the wilderness; why have you brought us to this land? Let us choose a leader and return to Egypt."

But Caleb and Joshua said, "The land is good; if God delights in us, He will give us the land and victory. Do not fear, and have faith that the Lord will help us possess the land." The people didn't listen to them and rebelled. They wanted to stone them. They defied God, and He said, "They will never enter my Promised Land."

Due to their rebellion, they lost the gift of paradise. Caleb and Joshua believed in God, and He rewarded them with paradise.

2. Rebellion brings humiliation and death

Antiochus IV Epiphanes had everything in life. He had power, wealth, and he glorified himself above God. He did not do what was right in the sight of the Lord, and he said, "I will make Jerusalem a cemetery of Jews." He persecuted the Jewish people. He defiled the temple by entering it and dedicating it to Zeus, the Greek god. He mocked God and defiled the temple by sacrificing unclean animals. He rebelled against God; he mocked His holiness. God struck him with an illness, and he smelled very bad. His servants could not bear him as his flesh was rotting, and his body was infested with worms. Rebellion brought him a horrible death.

Always be subject to God and never think of yourself as equal or greater than God.

However, even in moments of disobedience, God's mercy is available.

3. Even in moments of disobedience God's mercy is available

God's mercy endures forever, and even though we don't deserve it, His mercy is endless. He is always waiting for us to come back to Him, so we can experience His mercy.

God created Adam and Eve, and He gave them the gift of paradise. He gave them His image and likeness. He gave them dominion over all the creatures of the earth and even allowed them to name all creatures. He did so much for them and gave them only one commandment: "Do not eat the fruit from the tree of knowledge." They did not obey God, and they came to see that they were naked after eating the fruit. They had to get fig leaves to cover themselves. God was angry with them, no doubt about it. But He provided them with clothes. That is the mercy of God.

They rebelled against Him for forty years, and God still gave them the Promised Land. Throughout humanity, we have continued to push God away and have rebelled against Him. Through His unwavering mercy, He sent us his only begotten son Jesus Christ, to save us. His mercy and grace are always available to us. So, instead of rebelling against God, let us surrender to His will!

16. Rimmon Parez: Access to God

From Rithmah, they traveled to Rimmon Parez. Which means, God breaks all barriers and gives access to God.

The Israelites were grumbling, questioning, and doubting God. They sinned against God, and they abandoned Him numerous times. They had so many barriers against God, and He broke all of them, giving them access to His love and mercy.

1. People who began with God and ended with God

a. Six million Israelites had access to God, and due to their pride and sinfulness, most of them lost access to God. On the other hand, Caleb and Joshua had complete and everlasting access to God, from the beginning to the end. Starting with God is vital, but it is more important to be in His good graces at the end. This is vital in order to be with Him for eternity.

b. Jehoida, the high priest, began with God and ended with Him. Jehoida anointed Joash as the king of Judah. He commanded all the officers to protect the king and to accompany him at all times. Athalia learned this and said that they were being disloyal. She shouted, "Treason, treason." So, the high priest Jehoiada commanded the captains to kill her, and they did as he commanded. The high priest tore down the altars and all the images of Baal. He had Mattan, the priest of Baal, killed before the altars. Joash restored the temple of God! Jehoida, the high priest, led Joash and helped him walk in the path of God.

Jehoiada passed away at the age of 130 years. He received the highest honor and farewell. They buried him in the city of David among the kings because he did so much good for the Israelites, for God, and the temple of the Lord.

2. Those who began with God and ended without God

Hezekiah lived a righteous life and did what was pleasing to God. He became a king when the people completely forgot about God, and they indulged in all kinds of evil. He took charge and brought about so much transformation, and he restored the temple of God and brought back faith to the people.

a. God did wonders in the life of Hezekiah

God won battles for Hezekiah (angels struck down 185,000 Assyrians). When he was sick, he cried out to the Lord. And through the prophet Isaiah, God granted him healing and extended his life by fifteen years.

Ended with judgment

The Babylonians heard that King Hezekiah was sick and came to visit him. Instead of taking in the miracle of God's healing, he boasted about his achievements and his wealth. He showed them all his treasures: the silver, the gold, the spices, the precious oils, and his armory. He showed them everything in his house. Isaiah came to him and said, "Since you boast about your success, all of it will be taken away from you and taken to the Babylonian kingdom." Hezekiah ended his life in judgment. Wealth can distract us and take us far from God.

b. Demas began with God and ended without Him

Demas was a fellow worker of St. Paul. He was doing God's work, but he was seeking attention and recognition. He did not get what he wanted, and that is why Paul writes, "Demas loves the things of this world, and he has deserted me. He has gone to Thessalonica. He began with God and ended with the world; he has lost our Lord forever."

3. Those who began without God and ended with God

Onesimus was a servant to Philemon. He was caught stealing, and he tried to flee. He ended up in prison with Paul. From prison, Paul wrote to Philemon appealing for him to forgive Onesimus. He said, "he was unprofitable, but now he is profitable. Please accept him. I know he has wronged you, and if he owes you anything, I will repay it on his behalf. Please accept him." He began without God and ended in God's favor.

17. Libnah: Holiness

God's will for each one of us is to be holy and avoid immorality, especially sins of the flesh. We will battle temptations daily; we need to keep our minds, hearts, and bodies pure. It is through our holiness that Jesus Christ will grant us access to Heaven.

1. Mind

When we have God's word in our minds and when we meditate on scripture, it will keep us away from sin. A man of God from Judah came to Bethel and warned Jeroboam, who was worshiping at the altar. He said, "Josiah from the house of David will destroy this altar." He prophesied that one day the altar would be torn apart, and the king became angry. Jeroboam stretched out his hand against a man of God and commanded his men to seize the man. The hand that he stretched out dried, and he could not draw it back. Later, the man of God prayed, and the king received healing. Because of his prayers, the king invited the man of God to his house. The king promised a reward, but the man of God said, "Even if you give me half of your wealth, I will not come with you. The Lord commanded me not to eat or drink, but rather asked me to return the same way I came." When we have the Word in us, it will keep us away from sin (1 Kings 13:1–10).

2. Heart

When David was old and wise in years, they covered the king with clothes but did not give him warmth. They searched the entire territory of Israel and brought a beautiful young girl named Abishag to give warmth and to care for him, but he did not sin with her (1 Kings 1:1–4). When our hearts long for God, it will help us remain holy.

3. Body

St. Paul writes in his letter, "desires of the flesh are against the spirit. Clothe yourself with Jesus Christ and never feed flesh with desires." He warns Timothy to be holy so that he may be a vessel for noble use, consecrated and useful to the master's house, ready for good work. Keep yourself away from your youthful passions and aim at righteousness.

When we keep the body, mind, and soul pure, God will give us:

a. **Testimony:** The prophet Zechariah had a vision about Joshua the high priest. He was standing before the angel of the Lord, and Satan was ready to accuse him. God rebuked Satan as in the case of Moses' body, saying he was a burning stick plucked from fire, and he was saved from the world of desires, like Judah was saved from exile.

b. **Fine garments:** Joshua was standing before the Lord with filthy garments, and the angel of the Lord said, "Remove the filthy garments and clothe him with rich apparel and a clean turban placed on his head." This showed that he was purified from his impurity and made holy and fit for the Lord forever.

c. **Crown:** God told Zechariah to make a crown and place it on the head of Joshua the high priest. When we remain holy, God Himself will give us testimony, fine garments, and a crown.

18. Rissah: Jew - Mercy

The Israelites traveled from Libnah to Rissah, which means mercy.

1. The mercy of God turns our mess into a message

I'm sure most of us have heard the story of the "Prodigal Son." He loved his father and was obedient to him when he was young. Later in life, he demanded his inheritance early and abandoned his father. In the beginning, everything was great, and he was enjoying himself with all his wealth. He eventually depleted all his wealth. He was broken, all of his friends abandoned him, and he had nothing left.

There are two things that happened at the same time in this story:

a. He wasted all his money on worldly pleasures and was left with nothing.

b. A great famine hit the city.

Blow after blow, strike after strike; he was betrayed by his friends, he was frustrated, hungry, and it hit him all at once.

Just imagine if there were no famine in the city; he would have possibly found a job and never returned home to his father.

But God brought these two situations together at the same time. The "Prodigal Son" had no choice but to think of his father and how blessed he was when he was in his father's good graces. God created a situation that made him deal with the reality of his circumstances.

And he realizes two things:

a. His foolish mistakes.

b. His father's mercy.

He repented and wanted to return to his father's house; he wanted to reconcile himself with his father. As he was approaching his childhood home, his father recognized him from far away. He ran to him, hugged him, and welcomed him home with open arms. He was filthy, stinky, and barely recognizable to others. His father knew who he was, and nothing mattered to him except his son's returning home. It brought so much joy that he had his servants prepare a feast. And this is how the mercy of God works.

2. Mercy matters

Mordecai was a good man; he adopted Esther as his daughter. He was bought as a slave by a Persian king. He was separated from his family and country. The king removed him from all he knew, and he took away all his happiness. Mordecai served at the gate as a watchman guarding the king and the empire. One day, he was taking a rest in the courtyard, and he overheard two Eunuchs planning to kill King Artaxerxes. After hearing this plot, he went to the king and exposed what he heard.

The King interrogated the Eunuchs, and he found that Mordecai was truthful, and he executed the Eunuchs. Mordecai thought mercy was better than vengeance, as he always did what was right in the eyes of God. Jesus said, "Love your enemies, do good to those who hate you, and pray for those who persecute you." This is how Mordecai lived. He saved the person who made him a slave, and he served the king, who persecuted him, honorably. Mercy is the pathway to a better life here on earth and a key to the gates of Heaven.

3. The mercy of God that gives us hope

The Lord made a covenant with Abraham about the Canaan land. Abraham said, "How can I know that I will possess this land?" and God gave him proof.

"Bring me a heifer that is three years old, a goat that is three years old, a ram that is three years old, a turtledove, and a young pigeon."

He brought them and cut them in two, except the birds. He protected them from danger. As Abraham fell asleep, God said, "Your descendants will be slaves in a foreign land, and later they will possess the land."

When the sun set, it was dark. A smoking fire pot and flaming torch passed between the halves of the animals, and God solidified the covenant with Abraham.

This is how people made a binding covenant. If either of them broke the covenant, they would be cut in two like the animals. God was telling Abraham that if either of them failed to keep the covenant or if his people failed to keep the covenant, He would take their place. Years passed, and many people broke the covenant. The Lamb of God took our place, and He died for our sins. He took our curse upon Himself and suffered greatly. This is the mercy of God! He gives us hope, and He gives us so many opportunities to remain in His good graces. Death is not the end; we have hope of the resurrection through Christ.

19. Kehelathah - Worship

The Israelites had different experiences as they traveled to Kehelathah.

1. The faith of Judith transformed a pagan, who was an Ammonite

After hearing and seeing the miracles the Lord did for the Israelites. Others became believers in God, and one of them was Achior, a pagan who was an Ammonite. Achior knew about the Israelites and about their God. He expressed that knowledge to a mighty warrior, Holofernes. He said, "You may have strength, power, and an army, but you cannot defeat the Israelites if they remain loyal and faithful to their God."

Holofernes did not take his words seriously and mocked him, saying, "After defeating the Israelites, I will put an end to your life." God gave victory through the courageous widow Judith. Achior saw the head of Holofernes in her hand, and he became a strong believer in God.

2. Worship transformed a family

St. Paul and Silas were on their way in prayer. A slave girl who was possessed followed them and cried out, "These men are servants of God. They proclaim the way to salvation." She was doing this for several days, and Paul was annoyed.

He said, "In the name of Jesus, I command you to come out of her," and the demon left her immediately. The slave's owner brought charges against them, and a crowd attacked Paul and Silas. The magistrates tore their garments and ordered the crowd to beat them. After inflicting physical punishment, they were imprisoned. In the middle of the night, they were heard worshiping God, singing hymns of praise, and miracles transpired.

a. There was a great earthquake.

b. The foundation of the prison was shaken.

c. All the prison doors were opened.

d. All the chains fell off the prisoners.

Seeing all these things, the guard was about to take his own life. Paul said to him, "Don't harm yourself. No one has escaped; we are all here."

He fell before Paul and Silas and said, "What must I do to be saved?"

Paul said, "Believe in Jesus Christ; you and your household will be saved."

Their worship changed the guard's entire family.

3. Matthias' faith transformed his entire community

Matthias was a great leader and well respected in the city. He lived for his faith and led his family to walk in faith. The king's officer commanded Matthias to obey the commands of the king above God's. The officer said, "By doing this, you will be a friend of the king and your family will be honored with gold and silver."

Matthias responded and said, "Even if the entire people abandon their religion and obey the king, my family and I will always live the covenant of my forefathers."

One Jew abandoned his faith and offered a pagan sacrifice in Modein. Matthias was enraged and killed him and the officer. He said, "All those who love the law and the covenant come with me." They all moved with faith and went with him.

One man's faith transformed the entire community.

4. The prophet Daniel changed an entire nation

Daniel lived in faith and always remained loyal to God, even in exile. He was honored for all his counsel and won the favor of the king. Some officers who were against Daniel planned a plot against him, and they manipulated the king into passing a decree that stated whoever prayed to God and not the king should be put into the den of lions. Daniel did not care about the decree and kept praying to God and only God. He prayed three times a day! So, the officers brought charges against Daniel, and the king sent him into the den of lions.

The king said to Daniel, "May your God whom you serve continually deliver you." God saved Daniel from being mauled by the lions, and after seeing this miracle, King Darius created a new decree that said, "In all my royal dominion, men will tremble and fear the God of Daniel, for He is a living God."

One man's faith transformed an entire nation.

20. Mount Shepher: The Glory of God

Mountains are always seen as a place that is close to God and a place of prayer and glory. Mount Shepher means brightness. The Israelites experienced the glory of God throughout their entire journey. The Israelites abandoned God in their times of trouble, but His glory never left them; it remained with them constantly.

1. Obedience brings glory to God forever

After many years of patience and faithfulness, the promise of God was fulfilled, and Abraham finally received his own child. He was so happy, and Sarah praised God for this blessing as well. In that joyful moment, God came to Abraham and requested that he offer his only son, Isaac, as a sacrifice on Mount Moriah. He walked three days up the mountain, and in those three days, he never questioned God or expressed his sorrow. He believed in God and had faith in His plan. He obeyed God and was willing to sacrifice his own son. While he was about to come down and strike Isaac, God stopped him and provided a sacrificial offering in place of his son.

After many years, God rewarded Abraham for his obedience. Through King Solomon, He had a temple built. It was built on the same spot where Abraham was about to sacrifice his only son. Abraham's obedience carried the glory of God forever.

2. King David longed for God; the glory of God remained with him forever

God loved Saul and made him the first king of Israel. God protected Saul and gave him many victories. But Saul did not revere God; he pursued wealth, power, and fame. Because of Saul's disobedience, God's grace departed from him. The Ark of the Covenant was taken by the Philistines, and he lost his favor with God forever.

King David longed for God all his life. He knew the importance of God's presence and favor. King David thought that he could accomplish anything with God. But with God, he could do great things. So, he went after the Ark of the Covenant and seized it from his enemies. King David danced and celebrated when he received the Ark of the Covenant.

King David loved the Lord and loved being in His presence, and God never left him. When we run after God and seek Him and all His glory, He will always remain with us.

3. Gratitude will bring us close to the glory of God

In the gospels, we find that those who came with a problem found a solution. Those who came sick found healing, those who came with repentance found mercy. The weak found strength and the weary found peace. Jesus always answered their prayers. He always said yes to those who had faith in Him, and He worked wonders in their life. We see this when ten lepers came to Him for healing. He said to them, "Go to the priest," and while they were on their way, they were all healed. But among the ten, only one of them came back to Jesus with gratitude. Jesus praised the Samaritan who returned. The Samaritan had a gracious heart. He touched the feet of Jesus and felt the glory of God. The other nine lost their chance of touching Jesus and feeling His glory because they didn't have a gracious heart.

Have a gracious heart, and you too will have an opportunity to touch and to feel the glory of God.

21. Haradah: Fear of God

The Israelites traveled many miles, and they reached Haradah, the halfway point to the Canaan land. The meaning of the name Haradah is "The fear of the Lord." The psalmist said, "God looked from Heaven, and he found no one who had the fear of God on earth."

Fear of the Lord is the fountain of life. All those who fear the Lord will find meaning and life in abundance. A lot of righteous people left letters and messages proclaiming their fear of God.

1. King David's farewell speech

King David, at the end of his life, said to Solomon, "My son, fear the Lord all your life, with all your heart and soul, walk in His ways, follow all His statutes, commandments, ordinances, and testimonies so that you will have prosperity and life wherever you go."

2. Samuel's farewell speech

"Israelites, pay heed to me and know the wonders of the Lord. Every time you feared and cried out to the Lord, He delivered you from your enemies. When your forefathers feared the Lord and cried out to Him, He sent Moses and Aaron and saved you from the Egyptians."

They cried out to the Lord, saying, "We have sinned and worshipped the gods of Baal and Ashtoreth."

"God sent Jerubbaal, Barak, Jephthah, and Samuel; you were delivered from your enemies and dwelt in safety. Therefore, fear the Lord, serve Him, listen to the voice of the Lord, and follow the commandments of the Lord. It will go well with you, and the hand of the Lord will be with you and your king."

Today, many people have forgotten the Lord and turned away from Him completely. All those who have abandoned God face danger and eternal damnation.

a. **The traveler who abandoned God**

In one of the gospels, Jesus mentions a traveler who journeyed from Jerusalem to Jericho.

Jerusalem is called the "City of God." For all the Israelites, it is known as the center of worship and prayer. He is leaving such a place and going down to Jericho.

Jericho is a place of danger, and it is cursed. Joshua cursed the city in the Old Testament.

This man abandoned the presence of God and traveled to Jericho. On his way there, he was beaten, stripped, robbed, and left to die on the side of the road. Even though he left God's presence, God did not leave him. Rather, he showed His love and mercy through the actions of the Good Samaritan.

b. **Shimei, who left Jerusalem**

Shimei had a very bad past, and he cursed David badly. One day, Solomon came and warned him to remain in Jerusalem. He said, "You will have life and safety."

He ignored the warning of King Solomon and left the city, and that decision led to his death.

God gives us warning after warning through His prophets, and those who heed will have life, and those who do not will suffer.

c. **Absolom left the king's presence**

Absalom was perfect in his appearance from head to toe, and people sang of his perfection. There wasn't

> another man in the entire region like him. Externally, he was perfect, but internally, he was flawed. In other words, he was spiritually impure. He rebelled against his father and murdered his brother. King David said, "Let him not in my presence." He lost the king's presence forever.

Beauty is a blessing, but it won't get us a seat at the King's table. Our heart and soul will earn us the greatest rewards imaginable. We need to always strive for spiritual perfection.

Conclusion

For the most part, every human being who journeys through this world wants to have a beautiful ending. When God called the Israelites from Egypt to the Promised Land, they had no idea where they were going; rather, they had faith and believed in God's promise. Six million Israelites began their journey to the Promised Land and only two of them made it to their destination. Starting the journey with faith is important, but completing the journey in union with God is imperative.

1. The Israelites began with God but most of them did not end with Him.
2. Caleb and Joshua began with God and ended with God.
3. Rahab the prostitute did not begin with God but ended with Him.

I pray this book helps you discern and/or strengthen your vocation; may it help you have steady faith in times of trouble, and I pray the Lord rewards you with a very blessed end.

I hope that after reading this book, it will compel you to spend more time with the Lord and it will become a habit for you. This practice will help you align your will to God's. Like a sunflower that is always directed to the sun, I pray you will always be directed to the God of Heaven and earth. When your journey in this world is complete, I pray the gates of the Promised Land (Heaven) will be open and you will hear the voice of God say, **"You are my beloved and I am well pleased with you!"**

Conclusion

About the Author

Reverend Father Bartholomew Nanduri, SAC

He was ordained to the priesthood on April 24, 2018, and belongs to the Society of the Catholic Apostolate (Pallottines). He served for seven years in India and is currently the Parochial Vicar at Sacred Heart Catholic Church in Wichita Falls in the Diocese of Fort Worth, Texas. He is grateful to God for his vocation and proud to be a Pallottine priest, joyfully serving God and the Church in the spirit of St. Vincent Pallotti.

Rivershore Books

www.rivershorebooks.com

info@rivershorebooks.com

Made in the USA
Coppell, TX
13 June 2026

81170316R10049